MW01705374

How I Discovered The Truth

To Evelyn.
Best wishes
John Cawsey
21 March 2011

How I Discovered The Truth

John Cawsey

Pearl Press

First published in Great Britain by Pearl Press Limited

ISBN 978-0-9565001-6-8

Printed and bound by Good News, Ongar, England.

Contents

Introduction

In 2003 I published a book entitled *My Search For The Truth*. This was the result of years of wondering why we are here. What is the truth behind everything we see? My conclusions suggested the Gods are having a game of chess in the sky and occasionally we get a glimpse of the chessboard. Can we get a closer look at the chessboard? I certainly have been able to. That's why I want you to read on.

My Background

From an early age my loves were piano playing and sailing. Adventures at sea came naturally from generations of sea captains, from my grandfather, great grandfather and from generations I have traced back to two pilgrim ships in 1605 and 1609 which sailed for Virginia to colonize America. The story of the seafarers from Appledore and Bideford, trading under sail, are well documented in the National Maritime Museum, Greenwich, London.

I showed an interest in my teens for astronomy and joined a local astronomical society. I bought a telescope with an 8.5 inch mirror and a strong mounting and began exploring the heavens.

What was out there in the sky?

Passing A Level subjects in Chemistry, Physics and Biology, I entered Bristol University to become a dental surgeon. My love of piano playing continued but the life of a concert pianist would be too difficult to achieve.

I practiced dental surgery for many years and spent as much time as I could afford adventuring on the sea. Going to sea on my father's yacht at an early age gave me some experience of handling a yacht. Navigation lessons followed and at the age of 22 I chartered a 38ft sailing yacht and took friends on a months cruise down the Bay of Biscay.

At the age of 25 I purchased my first yacht and sailed to France and the Channel Islands. In the winter I taught sailing and navigation at night-school classes, first the Day Skipper Certificate and later, Yachtmaster level. This led to a teaching career and a license issued by the Royal Yachting Association on behalf of the DTI to my sailing school, Cutlass Sailing School in 1969. I later obtained a license to teach shore based courses by distance learning for my Tiller Correspondence School.

In 1979 I built a 36ft yacht in my front garden for teaching with Cutlass Sailing School. In 1984 I sailed it across the Atlantic and back.

In 1997 I sailed back to the Caribbean and continued running sailing school courses in St Lucia.

In 2007 I sold my yacht in the Caribbean but continue teaching shore based courses of Day Skipper and Yachtmaster in the Island of Bequia. In this beautiful small island is a large bay, Admiralty Bay, with lots of yachts on moorings and at anchor. I bought a piano for St Mary's Anglican Church, where I give piano recitals and teach the boys and girls to play piano free of charge.

Sailing to the Island of Bequia in the Caribbean

Chapter One

Conclusions from my last book *My Search For The Truth*

This book took two years to write. I analysed a wide range of subjects from astronomy, cosmology, the Universe, formation of our planet, physics, Einstein, chemistry, biology, ecology, meteorology, global warming, the human brain, religions and unexplained phenomena. I subjected every subject to the following tests:

1 That a scientific experiment could be analysed and found to produce the same result on repetition, indicating it was proved in scientific terms.

2 A phenomenon is observed by many people that has a repeatable pattern but cannot be understood in scientific terms.

3 The judge summing up a case when he says 'The weight of evidence, is in favour of …..' An example of this would be the possible existence of millions of inhabited planets in the universe on a chance basis when the building blocks of life are already floating in cloud gases in the sky.

Of the many conclusions reached and questions raised, the important ones are:-

1 Order did not come from chaos - order has come from design. There is a design feature running through everything. Maybe everything is scientific but we don't know the sciences.

2 The common denominator is the beauty and diversity of creation.

3 The human brain has expanded in size three times in 2 million years giving it a computing power a million times greater. The reason for this is not known. Either we inherited it from a race 300,000 years ago or, by stimulation which has no scientific basis to understand, it just happened.

4 Energy came first and material forms were made from it. Energy and matter are interchangeable.

5 Many millions of planets are inhabited by energy and material forms.

6 In material construction we have inherited a Darwinism of organic chemistry. DNA has probably been in existence for five billion years. Has DNA been altered in all this time?

7 Could other intelligent life have landed on planet Earth?

8 How many millions of designers have contributed to designing planet Earth? Earth certainly seems to be a place for experimenting with creation, from making insects, fishes, birds, animal and human lives and plant and vegetable life. I think Earth is an experimental laboratory for growing things. Perhaps that is why UFOs come back every so often to see how their experiments are working.

There are many other conclusions I reached from my last book. There are many, many more conclusions I have reached from my new book. Would they be your conclusions if you had had the same experiences as me? Read on…..

Chapter Two

My Story - Meeting Verona - Jesus and Healing

My life has been an alternation between my love of piano playing, sailing the seas, teaching nautical subjects as a yacht master instructor and making a living as a dental surgeon.

In 1984/85 I took nine months off to do a transatlantic and back voyage covering 9000 miles in that time, while a locum dentist looked after my surgery.

By 1989 NHS dentistry had become unprofitable. The government didn't implement the independent review body's findings which recommended increasing dental practice expenses. Mrs. Thatcher's government increased patients' charges to 75% of the cost of treatments so patients didn't come. Forms to claim payment on completed work were computerised. You needed to take a course on computers to understand how to fill in the forms to get paid. Dentists went bankrupt. Now you can't find a NHS dentist - hardly surprising!

Luckily, in one sense, in 1989 I received a disability pension because of osteoarthritis in my right wrist.

Now I had plenty of time to run my sailing school and marine correspondence school.

In 1997 I set out again to return to the Caribbean. In September 1997 I crossed the Bay of Biscay and sailed to the Canary Islands. In late November I set off across the Atlantic on the Trade Winds and twenty-two days later, arrived at my favourite Caribbean island, Bequia, a small island south of St Vincent. However, I chose St Lucia as my base so I could continue my sailing school courses for my students. I flew back to England and returned after the hurricane season was over on 1st

December to continue teaching.

In 2003 I anchored off a very small island, Mayreau, 16 miles south of Bequia. I met Verona on the beach, a beautiful lady, bought her a drink in a bar and the next day invited her to sail away with me on my yacht to Bequia.

We fell in love.

Verona went back to Mayreau and made plans to come to England where I live in the fishing port of Brixham, South Devon.

Verona was a Shakespearian actress in San Fransisco. She was trained in London, met an American, married and went to live in Marin County, about 20 miles from the Golden Gate Bridge. Her husband died some years later, now she was arriving to stay with me in Brixham. I was very excited but not to hear the news when she arrived - she had breast cancer. Verona was operated on at Torbay hospital eleven days later. The oncologist said, 'You only have a 50/50 chance of living. This is a grade three most dangerous form of cancer and it has passed all operable lymph nodes.'

Verona had medical insurance in America and went home to receive all the available treatments. She rejoined me one year later in St Lucia and we sailed to Grenada.

One month later she was dying in my arms, with a massively swollen stomach. I flew her back to England to Torbay hospital. When I came home the oncologist had given her three months to live and was transferring her to Rowcroft nursing home. I questioned the oncologist about the cancer cells and doubted his findings. I suggested she was dying of cirrhosis of the liver. The liver experts confirmed I was right, and later Verona was flown back to America for more treatments. After a small operation Verona made a recovery sufficient to return to Brixham for a 6 week holiday. She had terminal liver failure and would die within three years.

My friends and I spent a lot of time caring for Verona and I went to San Fransisco to stay with her on two occasions. Now she was coming back to Brixham. I met her at Gatwick Airport near London, and we travelled by train to South Devon. Four Days later I took her to an open air concert. Because she could only walk a limited distance without getting exhausted I hired a wheelchair. Going down an artificial slope onto the grass, the wheelchair tipped upside down. Verona had face cuts but I pulled the disc out of my back between lumber four and five vertebrae.

We made the best of our holiday together. On 3rd August I put her on the aeroplane to America. On 4th August she went swimming in her swimming pool and hit her head going in. She drowned. I didn't know for a week because I had gone to Alnwick in Northumberland to play piano for my friend Elisabeth Northumberland and her family.

So much for a fairytale romance - Verona dead and me in a wheelchair.

I could get no treatment from my doctor in Brixham because he said the waiting list was too long. His advice was to go home and take pain killers - you're getting old.

I returned to Grenada, launched my yacht and put her alongside Grenada Yacht Club so I could walk ashore on the pontoon. One week later I was ambulanced to Grenada hospital unable to walk. I was x-rayed and told I had a spinal injury. The consultant orthopaedic surgeon was helpful and ordered rest. Whatever position I lay in there was bad pain, terrible at times, not for a day, not for a week, but month after month. I prayed to Jesus to help me. Thanks to my taxi driver Ken, I managed to get shopping and with the help of two newly acquired crutches, get back to my yacht.

On about 12th December at midday I got my groceries aboard and into the cockpit. I opened the washboard to go below and there was someone on the last starboard bunk only in outline shape, someone very tall.

There was a massive Holy Presence.

It was Jesus lying on the bunk as a comforter. The Holy Presence stayed aboard for two weeks. All I could do was to pray day and night. The experience changed my life. Little did I know then that I would meet Jesus again.

I made weekly visits to the orthopaedic surgeon and in March he said there were signs of recovery. I was still bent over spending too much time looking at the ground. With the help of a wheelchair service I went by local aeroplane to Bequia to listen to six brilliant musicians from the Royal Academy of Music in Oslo. These musicians had been before and included a lady opera singer. Marianne, who had arranged these concerts from Norway, bought an inexpensive piano and installed it in the church for a candlelit concert. Two days before the musicians were due to play I caught two local boys smashing up the piano. It couldn't be used. The concert went well without a piano.

I went back to Grenada, laid my yacht up ashore and flew home to England on 15th April 2006. I was met at Gatwick by my friend, Susan, who took me to her home on the Isle of Wight for two week's rest. I was still in much pain and on two crutches. My daughter, Francesca, suggested I went to a spiritual healer, which I did in Shanklin. It was a memorable experience, and a great white light flashed through my head. Three days later I was lying in bed one morning at Susan's when invisible hands lifted my leg off the bed, rotated my foot and felt my swollen ankle. I seemed to getting help from the Fourth Dimension. When I left Grenada, the consultant surgeon said I may have fractured my right foot and certainly the Achilles tendon was torn, and to get it x-rayed upon my return to Brixham. He also gave me a letter I posted to my doctor six weeks before my return saying I needed urgent treatment.

I returned to Brixham at the end of April but received no help from the doctors. I went on a waiting list for three weeks to be seen by a blind physiotherapist, who could eventually refer me to a consultant physiotherapist at Teignmouth, 15 miles away. Then a further referral would get me a consultant's interview after Christmas 2006, 9 months later.

I admitted myself to Torbay hospital for an x-ray of my very painful swollen right ankle. The x-ray indicated a fracture that had healed. In July I went privately to see the consultant orthopedic surgeon Mr Irvine at Torquay private hospital. A scan showed how far out the disc was from normal. Mr. Irvine said I only had a 50/50 chance of getting better. He recommended an injection between the vertebrae but not an operation, as I could be paralysed for life. I think this injection did help after many weeks.

In the meantime I prayed to Jesus and decided to do a course on spiritual healing and a second course on the healing properties of crystals and colour therapy. There are many ways leading to healing, starting with love and caring. I had read six volumes of books by Baird Spalding on journeys with the Masters of the Far East. These remarkable books I would recommend everyone to read. I would love to be a healer like Jesus. To be one I had to study, understand that God is purity, perfection, peace and love, and God abides inside all of us. God made the first perfect child called Christ. We are all descended from this perfect child, so we are all divine.

All negative words and thoughts must be abolished. For instance, there must be no hatred, no anger, no malice towards anyone. How difficult when I hated my doctor for not trying to help me! I continued with my course of spiritual healing and eventually we were allowed to practice on each other in the class.

On September 21st 2006 I was helping on Peace Day in the local hall in Brixham. Ladies had baked cakes and cookies to sell and many tables were laden with bric-a-brac. I was sharing table with a lady called Susie whom I had not met before. We were selling flowers and plant displays. The event was not well advertised as it was agreed to hold it at short notice. Hardly surprising only a few came and we raised only £285 for charity.

Susie was telling me about a two year university course she had completed in interesting spiritual matters. I was about to tell her about the terrible pain I had in my back and how Jesus appeared in the cabin on my yacht, when she stopped me and said, 'I know what you are going to say,' went red in the face and her mouth opened in an expression of astonishment. I asked what was wrong. She said, 'Jesus is standing behind you in the hall. He has an instrument and is working low down on your back.' So I stayed perfectly still. Susie went out of the hall to fetch her children from school and I packed unsold items and took a taxi home. Next day I left my crutches under the piano and never used them again, needing only a walking stick.

I thanked Jesus for healing me and, hardly surprising, I felt very spiritual and close to my friend Jesus. I was continuing my course on spiritual healing. I knew if I lived a perfect life of no negativity, thoughts of purity, perfection (which I achieve in one way playing my Steinway piano), peace and love to all, I could talk to Jesus anytime.

Jesus lives in the Celestial Realm, we call it the Seventh Dimension, in the invisible, but visible to each other. Grand Masters who have taken their body with them also live on the celestial realm. Jesus appears either in spirit or in His original body and can talk with you. He is tall, 6ft 2inches. He is surrounded by a beautiful white purple-like light which casts no shadows.

His spirit body is only an outline shape but can contain a Holy Presence. He may come in His own body to minister the sick and needy.

Baird Spalding and his eleven scientists spent three and a half years in Tibet, India and the Gobi Desert. Many times Jesus came, and with other Grand Masters, and they shook hands with Him, received instructions from Him, photographed Him, journeyed with Him. The photographs are in the Taw Cross Temple at Chungga Village, sealed away, but under Chinese control. Jesus said you must not worship the idol but the ideal. Jesus said when two or more are gathered together in My Name I shall be with you, in spirit or in person. I became so used to talking to Jesus and likewise today it is no different. I talk to Jesus like my brother and I tell Him I love Him. If I need His help I ask Him and He talks to me through my brain. If I ask correctly, I know the answer is yes before I have asked.

On this occasion I said to Jesus, 'I am going to have a party in my house on 17th November 2006. I am inviting a few friends from my spiritual healing class. Will you come to my party?' The answer was a yes, before I had even finished asking.

I said, 'The table will be laid with beautiful fish, salad, fruit and nuts. The log fire will keep us warm. I will play lovely music on my Steinway piano. Can you teach us about getting God within?'

Nine people came. The room was lit with background lighting and coloured chakra candles. I started teaching about close to God. My friend Susie came and was teaching two ladies sitting on the sofa. I realised a few people were not as good in their presentation as I had hoped. I promised Jesus I would make the occasion perfect and it was not. At 10 o'clock 4 people suddenly left.

At 10.15 Susie said, 'Jesus is in the garden.'

He then came in through my front door, touching Susie's arm, which tingled, entering the sitting-room and came to stand by my piano. Only Susie saw him as she is very clairvoyant, but two lady healers sitting on the sofa exclaimed that their healing hand were hot. Jesus left, leaving behind a feeling of peace. One year later the winter had taken its toll on the garden and nothing was left in bloom. About the first week of

November a lot of shrubs grew up each side of my path. By about 14th November a mass of flowers appeared each side of the path that Jesus had walked up one year before. They were real. I photographed them.

I returned to the Caribbean island of Bequia in November where I bought a piano for St Mary's Anglican Church. I give free piano recitals every day and the piano can be used for occasional concerts. I met a lovely lady from Barbados in her seventies, Sister Ann. She comes for a week's holiday to Bequia every year and stays at Julie's Guest House. Sister Ann has been to Buckingham Palace to collect her OBE for services rendered in Barbados.

She talks to Jesus very often. We talked over breakfast. She said Jesus was with us at the breakfast table and I knew it. When I talk to people about my experiences I sometimes find it hard to talk of these experiences. My vibrational energy rate goes up when I recall my experiences of being with Jesus. I know what Muslims mean when they say, 'We pray 5 times a day and have to prostrate ourselves before God because he talks to us. At Mecca God talks even more strongly to us.' One prayer at Mecca is equivalent to 100 prayers elsewhere. Gospel churches in the Caribbean have a higher energy level and it is interpreted as God talking to us.

It can be difficult to talk to people about your experiences. They class you as a lunatic or don't believe you, or say you are having psychological problems. I was invited to tell a Roman Catholic priest of my experiences. After 15 minutes he looked at his watch and said, 'When is your taxi coming?' I think the Pope dictates who has holy sacred experiences and it wasn't going to be my turn.

I have an elderly lady friend in Bequia who told me of an encounter with Jesus. Her first husband had a stroke and died 12 weeks later. She was so upset she could only cry. One morning sitting in bed a bright light came in the window and filled the room. The white light was so bright it obscured the room.

She said, 'Are you God?'

A voice said, 'Affirmative.'

Then Jesus appeared at the end of her bed and reassured her. She gave me a description of Jesus' face and lovely long hair to his shoulders. She said she was scared to tell anyone in case she was taken away in a psychiatrist's van to hospital.

There are problems in life which can come between you and Jesus. Hatred is one, having enemies, because you must forgive your enemies. Sometimes you hold a grudge against someone.

I wrote to the Prime Minister saying, 'You wouldn't treat a dog as badly as I have been treated.'

It was left up to me to take legal action against my doctor. Top solicitors on claims for negligence said you will probably get £3000 damages but it will cost you £30,000. So I gave up the idea of vengeance and closed the file. I was relieved of my burden of negativity and I could make contact with Jesus again.

I found good advice in 'The Dalai Lama's book of wisdom'. He knows how to cope with great sorrow and stress. When you see things going wrong and you are powerless to do anything you become frustrated and this upsets your inner peace. Go for a walk and look at the beautiful flowers, which God has made for you to enjoy; look at the beautiful birds that fly around you, the beautiful fishes in the sea, the beauty of nature. Then say, 'Thank you God for all these wonderful things for me to love,' be grateful for a little and think of others and help them. God will reward you.

Picture of services in St Mary's Anglican church

Chapter Three

The human brain - the real truth behind what the human brain can do

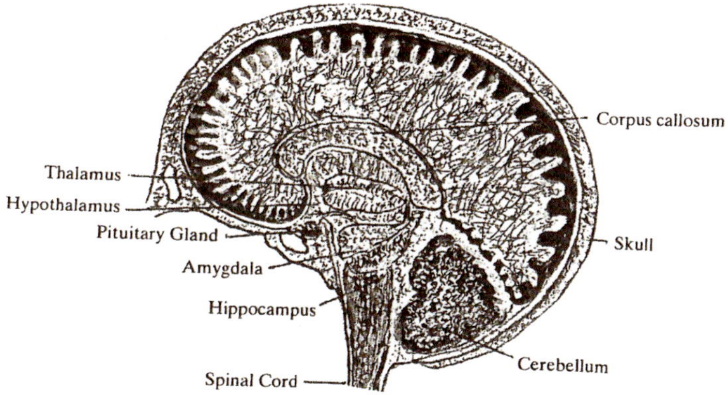

Five million years ago man and chimp were almost identical. Today a baby chimpanzee displays the same characteristics as a baby human. What caused the difference in chimp and human brains? The only clues I can think are:

1) The chimp learnt to climb trees to escape dangers. He developed simple language but never developed a specialised speech neuronal circuitry.

2) Man on the ground needed to make spears and sharp tools to defend himself, to learn how to use his hands, and the need to communicate by speech. Children may have invented more words and more signs to communicate with their parents. The development of a specialised speech

centre and modifications to the human voice box could have been the stimulus to start changes.

Two million years ago man had a small brain and lived in Africa and South East Asia. His primitive lifestyle did not require a bigger brain to operate his functions. The brain has increased three times in size in two million years and was nearly fully formed 200,000 years ago. Either we inherited our big brain from a superior race or, for reasons unknown, it expanded to this new size. Its computing power is now a million times greater, and it allows us to have syntax, the ability to join words into sentences for recalling, to reason, to plan ahead, to arrive at conclusions. No other creature on planet Earth can plan ahead for weeks at a time.

In my last book, *The Search for the Truth* I examined how the brain stored memory for recalling, how the brain learned to memorise patterns and in practical terms I illustrated how we learn to drive a car and play the piano; also the functions of different parts of the brain.

Learning comes from hearing, seeing, writing, feeling and from being shown, resulting in much repetition to produce memory patterns for recalling. If you examine the intelligence of a boy of 17 years, who cannot read or write, whose parents cannot read or write and Grandparents cannot read or write, it is very difficult for the boy to grasp the meaning and react to tasks because the brain has so little input for recalling. It's no good having a large brain if you don't use it. You need three generations of reading and writing to store sufficient memory to pass on intelligent genes. Once established hereditary can pass on intelligent genes for centuries.

A friend of mine is a descendant of John Field who taught Chopin how to write nocturnes in 1820. Paintings of John Field show a great likeness to his great, great, great, grandson, and my friend can show his inherited talent for music when he plays the guitar.

Intelligence is related to brain size and density of neuron connections, and the ability to use it. Einstein didn't have a large brain but more neuron connectors. Humans have more neuron connections in the visual cortex. We develop our brains by laying down memory patterns for recalling. The billions of circuits of nerve cells are interconnected or joined together at synapses. Neurotransmitters relay the signals across the synapses.

These are chemical connectors which are very highly sophisticated, enabling us too have rapid response in our human computer. The human brain can alter its internal circuitry to respond to change in environment; a manmade computer is programmed to give a response.

Two remarkable things have happened to man's brain. Neither of these things could have happened by Darwin's Theory or a natural progression along the lines of development.

1) The pharynx altered and the larynx adapted to form vocal cords with modifications to the tongue. The much longer pharynx makes possible the full range of sounds in articulate speech. This resulted 200,000 years ago in a voice box to produce speech. 2) At the same time the human brain increased in size and by 200,000 years ago, it was three times its former size two million years ago. This enabled us to construct words into sentences for recalling called syntax.

Now, with voice for communication and the ability to reason and plan ahead, we could understand the world about us and the science of the Universe. The Creator wanted to share His knowledge of creation. Perhaps next He will want us to create. We have strong evidence that intelligent man was present 200,000 years ago (see Chapter 4, The Baird Spalding Story).

Other functions of the human brain

1 Receiving sensory input from the body.
2 Computing the information against stored memory.
3 Sending impulses down the longer and thicker motor neuron fibres to every part of the body.
4 Storage of memory.
5 Transmitting power.
6 Communications by telepathy.
7 Receiving cells from the Divine Mind.
8 Maintenance of bodily functions and endocrines, through kundali lines connecting chakras and the etheric aura to our brain.

The basal part of the brain is the cerebellum at the top of the spinal cord, which is a sorting house for basic impulses.

The brain is in two halves and the right side of the body is represented on the left side of the brain. The two halves are joined at the decussating of the pyramids, which are at the top of the brain.

Individual areas are given over the specific functions e.g. vision from the optical nerve is represented at the back of the brain. In any large response from the brain, all the brain is used in computing power.

In the world of spiritual healing, we are told the left side of the brain is for logic, right side inspirational.

We all have a music centre in out brains. It is small. A musician can develop these cells and involve a much larger part of the brain. When I see a concert pianist sight reading pages of music with thousands of notes and instantly converting sight memory into finger memory, I think, what other wonders can the brain perform that we don't know? It does things without us realising it, like co-coordinating all the bodily functions and endocrine glands.

The eye records like a photograph. It fixes the picture and then it can send it out at the same rate of vibration at which the pictures were received. The same thing happens with thought and the spoken word. Each selective set of brain cells records and projects exactly as received. Another set of brain cells can record and fix the vibrations of other people's thoughts and pictures that other bodies or forms send out. You can send them back and assist others as well as yourself to control these thoughts. If a thought is immediately withdrawn it will not be fixed for transmission.

There are brain cells that receive the vibrations of the thoughts and activities of the Divine Mind. We do not have the Divine Mind, but we do have the cells that receive and project the vibrations of the Divine Mind. From this knowledge comes the understanding of vibrational energy rates which come from the Universal Substance and permeate everything. This is the while light of God, the spiritual energy that enters everything, under the control of universal laws. The seed produces the perfect flower. Its own vibrational energy comes from the universal substance and stays with it for the life of the plant.

The great scientist Sir Jagadish Chandra Bose of the Bose Institute, Calcutta, measured vibrational energy rates. He said plants have the lowest vibrational energy rate, animals a higher level and Man the highest level. He said the thought transmitting process could send out positive thought at 20,000 times the speed of light.

The Transmitting Power of the Brain

The Hindus say the thought is more powerful than the spoken word. It travels outwards at incredible speeds outside known sciences in a different medium. Distant healers can use this power to heal people at any distance. Harry Edwards was famous for his ability to heal people at a distance and also Betty Shine. Matthew Manning is still with us and demonstrating distant healing on people as far away as Australia. With over 150 cases documented by doctors where healing has taken place we see the power of positive thought and the proof healing has taken place.

Communication by Telepathy over Long Distances

Hindus train their brains to transmit and receive thoughts from a distance. Our brain can generate enormous power for transmissions. When we use our mobile phones every day it is reasonable to conceive we could train our brains to do the same. Soul to soul contact is called ATMA. I believe it won't be long before we can raise the vibrational energy level at the top of our heads and communicate with a higher dimension; perhaps we can do it already. There are remarkable people in the world that can do that, and display connections with the next life. They seem to be able to make bigger use of the electro magnetic spectrum. Often this gift runs in families and mediums demonstrate the gift in clairvoyance.

I went to a lecture by Divaldo Pereira Franco, a remarkable man who spent his boyhood playing with children from another dimension, and demonstrating his ability to talk and see into another dimension. His life work has been raising money to feed and educate the poor and giving lectures and assistance to world leaders. At the lecture he told us about an occasion when he was doing Divine Spiritual healing, and the neuroscientists were doing tests and photography on the brains of epileptics. On the photographs a small white light appeared at the top of the brain, the crown chakra during divine spiritual healing and has been photographed on Kirlian photography.

The British museum acquired the Gospel of Judas, and translation of the Coptic in 2006 revealed some additional teachings of Jesus. He says we do have connections to the Divine Mind in our brains.

Summary

I believe we have lost some of our spiritual connections with the Divine Mind due to our increasingly material existence, which has led to grave mistakes. I am talking about world leaders who have acted out the philosophy of man's supremacy and atheism, dictatorship and lack of human kindness to his fellow man. Do we have to have wars, atrocities by the millions? Isn't the writing on the wall when the human brain can contact God, who loves all of us, and we are His Divine children by hereditary from the perfect child, The Christ.

Isn't it time we controlled negative thoughts of hatred, anger, and substitute love to all nations?

Use your brain by fixing your thoughts on God and His Divine Perfection. Use your heart to love God and thank Him for the beauty of flowers and all nature He has made for us to enjoy. Continue praising God and this will raise the vibrations from the top of your head and you can connect with the Divine Perfection of God. Planet Earth has been an experimental laboratory for growing everything. Now with our large brains we can understand God's creation and realise everything is science under universal laws, a science of the spiritual world we have yet to learn.

Chapter Four

Forenote to Baird Spalding's Books Volumes 1, 2 and 3, *Voyages With Masters of the Far East by John Cawsey.*

Baird Spalding was a mining engineer, an author, who also wrote short stories, an expert in the Bible, with a knowledge of metaphysics. His family had lived in India for 300 years. Because the records of his voyages, maps, photographs, have not been found, there is no concrete proof he undertook all these voyages himself. They may be records of other people's voyages. The spiritual messages behind the books is enormous and illuminates the reason for the sale of millions of copies, which have helped so many people. It is like a reenactment of The New Testament; grand masters do exist.

Every few centuries we have miraculous happenings. This leads to prophecy for the future, and this is the way it has always been. The Bible is full of prophecy and when it comes true it illustrates God's work on Earth. Change is normal, everything moves on, hopefully for the better. This adds to intelligence, that mankind will find the perfection to enter God's kingdom.

Baird Spalding documented his voyages with Masters of the Far East. There is a legend in India of lost cities in the Gobi Desert of great antiquity and spiritual knowledge. The events leading to how to find these cities buried under tons of sand are a revelation in themselves. The help he and his group received from Grand Masters, mainly in India and Tibet, are miraculous. Baird qualified as a mining engineer and in archaeology working all over the world. He was a recognised expert on the Bible.

The years he spent with his eleven scientists working with help from the Grand Masters and Jesus, crossing Tibet to the Gobi Desert, are recorded in six small volumes of spiritual knowledge. Will the truth be revealed at a later date when all the photographs which his party took of the healings, voyages with the Grand Masters and Jesus are recovered from Taw Cross Temple? Jesus didn't want them published at that time and Jesus said you must worship the ideal and not the idol.

On lecture tours over many years Baird Spalding was asked repeatedly, 'Did you really see and talk with Jesus?'

His reply, 'Everything recorded in my books is true; yes we did.'

All the people helping them in their voyages displayed spiritual qualities, mostly people that have attained Mastership and taken their bodies with them enabling them to come and go in their bodies as they wished. In this way they spent their lives helping others both by healing and teaching.

Voyaging across Tibet and the Himalayas was at times difficult and dangerous. Many people helped them prepare voyages, short ones to temples and villages in the first year, and long ones across the Himalayas to the Gobi Desert. At times there were as many as 200 people in their party carrying tents, food, equipment, water, yaks to help carry everything, mountain passes to negotiate, swollen rivers to cross and terrible storms, and bandit countries. Phenomenal physical abilities were demonstrated and what seemed like ordinary everyday experiences to them, like walking on the water, were miracles to the Western world.

Baird Spalding's team of eleven scientists had cameras and could record what happened as they were trained in shorthand. They were sceptical and not easily convinced. They came away convinced of the extraordinary life of the Grand Masters and acknowledged that so many unexplainable things had happened. Their host, Emil, explained how some things were achieved. Jesus said everything is scientific but you don't understand the science. Baird and the eleven scientists photographed everything.

He said, 'They are real photographs,' because psychic matters do not come out on camera. In Tibet at high altitudes there was no electricity, no lighting, but lights came on when you went indoors. Your body made the light. Corridors went dark behind you.

The message was the same, 'The message is the manifestation by positive thought of achievement.'

Baird Spalding was born on a farm in upstate New York and at the age of four went to England. He attended preparatory school in Calcutta. He went to university at the Bose Institute completing studies by the age of seventeen. He went to California for two years more studying in Engineering and Archeology at Berkeley and Stanford. He qualified in mining engineering, archaeology and science. He worked all over the world in mining. Baird came from a family who had lived and worked in India for 300 years. He was a recognised expert on the Bible, and tracing the history of ancient civilisations and Jewish ancestry.

The background to the writings and voyages by Baird T Spalding in 6 volumes *Life and Teachings of the Masters of the Far East.*

(DeVorss & Co Publisher, PO Box 1389 Camarelllo, CA93011-1389) USA ISBN 087516 5389

I refer to these texts by kind permission from DeVorss & Co Publishers. www.devorss.com

There were stories in India of a very ancient city that once flourished in the Gobi Desert in the days when the Gobi Desert was a fertile area before the climate changed. His great grandfather made an exciting discovery when he was taking goods down the Ganges in the flood season. Water levels were high, currents very strong, destroying the river banks, and the boats were beached. One boat was alongside an exposed wall. They knocked a hole in the wall and found a vault. Inside were gold objects and a book bound in gold. The book appeared to be a reference book revealing there were four other books could be found in India with details of the lost cities with map references to latitude and longitude and distance and bearings.

Baird's grandfather went there in 1868. In 1895/96 the eleven scientists crossed the Tibetan plateau to the Gobi Desert, some 800 miles, and sank one mine shaft at 90ft and two at 45ft. They found the lost cities and opened vaults in good preservation. Findings indicated a well developed civilisation living in the spiritual side of life 200,000 BC.

Now I will go back to when the eleven scientists arrived in Calcutta in 1894 to prepare for the great Voyages ahead of them. The first year of planning the voyage to the Gobi proved to be very difficult. Baird Spalding was walking in the park in Calcutta and met Emil who offered valuable help in planning voyages. Emil displayed unusual gifts of foresight and Baird Spalding later found Emil to be a Grand Master sent to help him and his team. The first year was spent exploring temples and short journeys in Tibet, and living with Emil's friends in the Giama Nu Chu Valley. This gave them time to acclimatise to the high altitudes and where they were living at 11,600ft.

Emil appeared behind locked doors, could do body transfers 100 miles away, and explanations were given. It was obvious these people achieved things in different ways, a more natural way of life, but demonstrating the use of laws which came from another dimension. Baird Spalding summed up his feelings thus:

'There is no question but these people have bought the light through the long ages and they prove by their daily life and works that this light does exist just as it did thousands of years ago.'

The team were introduced to the Taw Cross Temple where ancient clay tablets, copies of the old Babylonian tablets were stored. A translator of the tablets gave them the chance to translate for themselves to get the best meanings. Jesus appeared in the temple, shook hands with them and gave them instruction. Also other Grand Masters came and taught them. All the Grand Masters had taken their bodies with them and could come and go at will for purposes of healing and teaching. When eventually the snow cleared in April, May of 1895 the whole expedition started on the long journey to the Gobi.

All of the voyages are recorded in volumes 1, 2 and 3. On their return to Darjeeling, the party of eleven scientists compared notes and conclusions. Baird Spalding returned to California and 3 of the scientists stayed in India to do more research work. Baird Spalding returned on 4th October 1935 with another party for a tour of the sacred sites in India. This produced book 4 which was written as a teaching aid based on his findings, and was called The India Tour. Volume 5 came from questions and answers of many years on lecture tours. Baird Spalding died in 1953.

Boxes of his writings were re-examined and more information contributed to volume 6 which was published in 1990. He outlived everyone, was always travelling, lecturing, and no personal friends are left to give accounts of the extraordinary man, a man who needed little sleep, a friend of many famous people, who left no possessions for he gave things away to help others. Baird's grandfather was very close to him and had the ability to take over and step into his body. This was probably agreed before he was born. Baird Spalding had acquired and displayed the ability to live close to his spiritual self.

He once said, talking about this wonderful civilisation that lived 200,000 years ago, 'The people accomplished more than we have accomplished today.'

I recommend you read volumes 1 - 6. I will finish by telling you of some everyday happenings which I expect you will term miracles. Emil appeared behind locked doors and explained how he did it. Lights came on without electricity. They travelled up the floors in the Taw Cross Temple by willpower or levitation. Chander Sen, the old man who translated the tablets, died. Jesus raised him from the dead. He came back as a young man of 45.

Emil could travel any distance in no time at all. He explained how he did it. They could project pictures on the walls of the temple showing past events and things to come (wars). When they set off at the end of April for the Gobi, they had to cross a swollen river running at 10 knots. 75 walked across the water. 75 trekked for 4 days up a mountain to cross by a bridge. A little girl gets Emil's mother to heal her little brother who had a bad accident. The little girl takes a blind lady to a meeting of many important people, and places her hands on the lady's eyes. Emil's mother steps forward and places her hands on the little girl. The blind lady sees after 25 years blind. Emil's mother rebuilt the little girl's mud hut with a lovely new house and clean clothes.

A trip to a healing temple where everyone is healed who believes. Bandits are repelled by magic and power. Levitation was demonstrated at the Pora Tat Sang Monastery. When they ran out of food on the way to the Gobi, the cooking pots were filled from universal substance. This couldn't be filmed, the cameras couldn't record it. A fire threatened to burn them alive. They raised their body vibrations and a hole opened up in the fire for them to pass through unharmed. When the natives were rowing them on a river, they stopped for lunch. A native fell asleep and his hand dropped in the water. A crocodile bit his hand off. Within 45 minutes a new hand had formed, so strong he carried on rowing. Other natives in the boat didn't consider this unusual.

Baird Spalding's scientists photographed the new hand forming. Jesus took the eleven scientists 'over the garden wall to see the next life.' One of the party leaders went to a village and proceeded to a jungle clearing outside. There on the ground was a body, which rose and joined into the leader's body. He had laid his own body down for the protection of the village some months before.

Behind the miracles lies a deep meaning, and many were not considered miracles but applying the universal law with a positive ability to create the result. Study all the effects and see if you can understand their cause and effect. Start with location, the ability to transfer your body to the desired end of your journey when you are very tired, by reading Psalm 23, and standing up in the knowledge you have reached the end of your journey. Try walking with feet and legs so light they hardly seemed to touch the ground. Imagine the distance you have to go is no real distance and that's why it is so joyful to complete. When you look back you will say my feet hardly seemed to touch the ground.

Chapter Five

Jesus' sayings - The Lord's Prayer - The thought process

God is spirit. We call it *the divine spirit* - it is everywhere. We need to draw it into ourselves, so we can use God from within. God is purity, perfection, peace and love. To reach God we need to raise our vibration energy very high from the top from the top of our head, the crown chakra. We can only do this if we are perfect.

It is necessary to list all bad words and never use them again of jealousy, anger, hatred. Use only positive thoughts and spoken words. In Hindu the thought is more powerful than the spoken word. In India, Tibet, Bhutan, there are many temples, some at great altitudes. In the great silence it is easier to contact God inside. This is why so many wondrous things happen in Tibet. When you have God inside of you, you can become a healer but you must operate in the knowledge of universal laws.

We have a spiritual body as well as a physical body. You can photograph the spiritual body on Kirlian photography. The secret of living this life is to live as close to the spiritual body as possible. Then there is no such thing as death. You cannot destroy the spiritual body; you take it with you into the next life, where everything carries on just the same. If you are very spiritual and good in this life you can take your body with you, the translation is literally 'over the garden fence'. You must achieve perfection in what you do. Every day be happy, give the perfect smile, enjoy the beautiful flowers. Talk to Jesus every day. Remember Jesus' three sayings.

1) 'Of myself I can do nothing. It is God inside me that does everything; you can do as I can do, and even greater things you can do.' We can heal like Jesus does.

2) 'When two or more are gathered together in my name I shall be in the midst of you. This will be in spirit, or in person.' Jesus says we live on the Celestial Realm. You call it seventh heaven, in the invisible, but visible to ourselves.

3) 'You shall know the truth and the truth shall make you free.' The great factor is divine understanding. God made *the Divine Christ* from which we are descended. So we are all *divine*, you must see the Divine Christ in every living soul. Everything on Planet Earth comes from a single cell, whether by photosynthesis, water, sunlight, pollination or a fertilised ovum. The single cell that blossoms into a flower is Divine.

A mighty oak tree, 100 years old, send forth new shoots, so young and beautiful, a replica of its youthful self. You will soon find that by fixing your thoughts and attention steadfastly on God, on His Divine perfection, you can raise the vibrations of your body so that they will blend so harmoniously with those of the Divine perfection that you are absolutely one with Divine Perfection and thus one with God. Only see perfection. Never see imperfection. When you have God's mind inside you a great white light will shine through your head.

Before consciousness existed there was Divine Truth. Man will be judged by comparing his conscious knowledge of the truth against absolute divine truth.

Jesus Christ said:

1) You shall love the Lord your God with all your heart, with all your soul, with all your mind and with all your strength.

2) You should love your neighbour as yourself.

With All My Heart:

I know from the depth of my heart you are my god, the father of all. You are purity, perfection, peace and love, from which flows the Truth. You have created all things, the beauty of flowers, of nature, birds, fishes, all things in the sea, on the land and in the sky. You are the life of my spirit. With your help I will make my intelligence your wish, to tell the truth to everyone, to spread the Gospel message as taught by your son Jesus Christ.

Beatitudes:- Jesus said 'Blessed are the pure in heart for the shall see God'

With All My Soul: (the soul and the spirit are the same)

Jesus planted a seed in my soul
Fed it with love so it would grow
Watered it daily from the fountain of life
And kept it away from all earthly strife
God's spirit is sure to take shape
And manifest in the holy place
For everyone to see
I am a divine tree
I have reached Christ consciousness
Which has set me free
Now I can say with the truest heart
I have reached out to God
Which is inside of me.

I now ask you, Father, to bring it forth, that I may express love, wisdom, strength and eternal youth, to receive harmony, happiness and abundant prosperity, and understand how to bring forth from the universal substance that which will satisfy every good desire.

With All My Mind:

God I hold my true desire in my mind with power and strength to project by my purest thoughts your every wish, that I may realise my oneness with you, and that I may give it out to everyone with your help.

With All My Strength:

With my faith, with all my strength, with my heart and with my desire I bring forth all I have asked for in your name God, that I now have your truth, love, wisdom, understanding, life, health, strength and eternal youthfulness. This gives me harmony, happiness and abundant prosperity in the knowledge I can seek every good desire from your love, the greatest word that the world must achieve.

The Most Famous Verse in the Bible

John 3.16 - 'For God so loved the world that he gave his only begotten son, that whoever believes in him shall not perish but have eternal life.'

Sermon on the Mount (The Beatitudes)

St Matthew - Chapter 5

The Beatitudes

'Now when He saw the crowds, He went upon a mountainside and sat down. His disciples came to Him and He began to teach them, saying,

'Blessed are the poor in spirit, for theirs is the kingdom of heaven.

Blessed are those who mourn, for they will be comforted.

Blessed are the meek, for they will inherit the earth.

Blessed are those who hunger and thirst for righteousness, for they will be filled.

Blessed are the merciful, for they will be shown mercy.

Blessed are the pure in heart, for they will see God.

Blessed are the peacemakers, for they will be called sons of God.

Blessed are those who are persecuted because of righteousness, for theirs is the kingdom of heaven.

Blessed are you when people insult you, persecute you and falsely say all kinds of evil against you because of Me. Rejoice and be glad, because great is your reward in heaven, for in the same way they persecuted the prophets who were before you."

The Lord's Prayer

The perfect prayer which includes Thanksgiving, Petition and Forgiveness. Here is the first request of the Lord's Prayer.

'Our Father who is in heaven
Let it be hallowed your name' (literal translation).

The Lord's Prayer begins with the Aramaic word Abba and therefore we can assume that Jesus taught his disciples to pray in Aramaic of daily communication rather than in the classical Hebrew of written texts. The Aramaic-speaking Jew in the first century was accustomed to recite his prayers in Hebrew, not Aramaic. Similarly, Muslim worshippers always recite their traditional prayers in the classical Arabic of seventh-century Arabia. Both Judaism and Islam have a sacred language. Christianity does not.

This fact is of enormous significance.

Jesus lived in a world where the public reading of the Bible was only in Hebrew, and prayers had to be offered in that language. When Jesus took the giant step of endorsing Aramaic as an acceptable language for prayer and worship, he opened the door for the New Testament to be written in Greek (not Hebrew) and then translated into other languages.

It follows that if there is no sacred language, there is no sacred culture. All of this is a natural outgrowth of the incarnation. If the word is translated from the divine to the human and becomes flesh, then the door is opened for that Word to again be translated into other cultures and languages. The long term result is a global church of more than two billion people, almost all of whom have the bible available in their own language.

Believers are thereby able to break into God's presence using the language of the heart. We are so accustomed to this heritage that we scarcely notice it's beginning, which was Jesus' choice of Aramaic as the language of the Lord's Prayer.

Luke's version of the Lord's Prayer opens with 'Father' while Matthew begins with 'Our Father.'

Both are legitimate translations of Abba.

The great Aramaic word affirms both respect in addressing a superior and a profound personal relationship between the one who uses it and the one addressed. It is easy to understand why the early Christian Church continued to use it even while praying in Greek. It invoked the quality of relationship the believer had with God through Christ. In this prayer God is our 'Father', nearby yet far away in 'heaven'. Just this one phrase of the great prayer teaches me God is 'Our Father' who is to be loved ad respected.

Anglicans in World Mission

Provinces of the Anglican Communion

1. The Anglican Church in Aotearoa, New Zealand & Polynesia
2. The Anglican Church of Australia
3. Igreja Episcopal Anglicana do Brasil
4. The Anglican Church of Burundi
5. The Anglican Church of Canada
6. The Church of the Province of Central Africa
7. Iglesia Anglicana de la Región Central de América
8. Province de L'Eglise Anglicane Du Congo
9. The Church of England
10. Hong Kong Sheng Kung Hui
11. The Church of the Province of the Indian Ocean
12. The Church of Ireland
13. Nippon Sei Ko Kai (The Anglican Communion in Japan)
14. The Episcopal Church in Jerusalem and the Middle East
15. The Anglican Church of Kenya
16. The Anglican Church of Korea
17. The Church of the Province of Melanesia
18. La Iglesia Anglicana de México
19. The Church of the Province of Myanmar (Burma)
20. The Church of Nigeria (Anglican Communion)
21. The Anglican Church of Papua New Guinea
22. The Episcopal Church in the Philippines
23. L'Eglise Episcopal au Rwanda
24. The Scottish Episcopal Church
25. The Church of the Province of South East Asia
26. Anglican Church of Southern Africa
27. Iglesia Anglicana del Cono Sur de América
28. The Episcopal Church of the Sudan
29. The Anglican Church of Tanzania
30. The Church of the Province of Uganda
31. The Episcopal Church (includes USA, parts of Europe, Haiti, Virgin Islands, Micronesia, Taiwan, Colombia, Dominican Republic, Ecuador Central, Ecuador Litoral, Honduras, Puerto Rico, Venezuela)
32. The Church in Wales
33. The Church of the Province of West Africa
34. The Church in the Province of the West Indies
35. Diocese in Europe, Church of England

United Churches

36. The Church of Bangladesh
37. The Church of North India
38. The Church of Pakistan
39. The Church of South India

Extra-Provincial Churches

40. Bermuda
41. The Church of Ceylon (Sri Lanka)
42. Iglesia Episcopal de Cuba
43. Falkland Islands
44. The Lusitanian Church
45. The Reformed Episcopal Church of Spain

Anglican Churches in the World

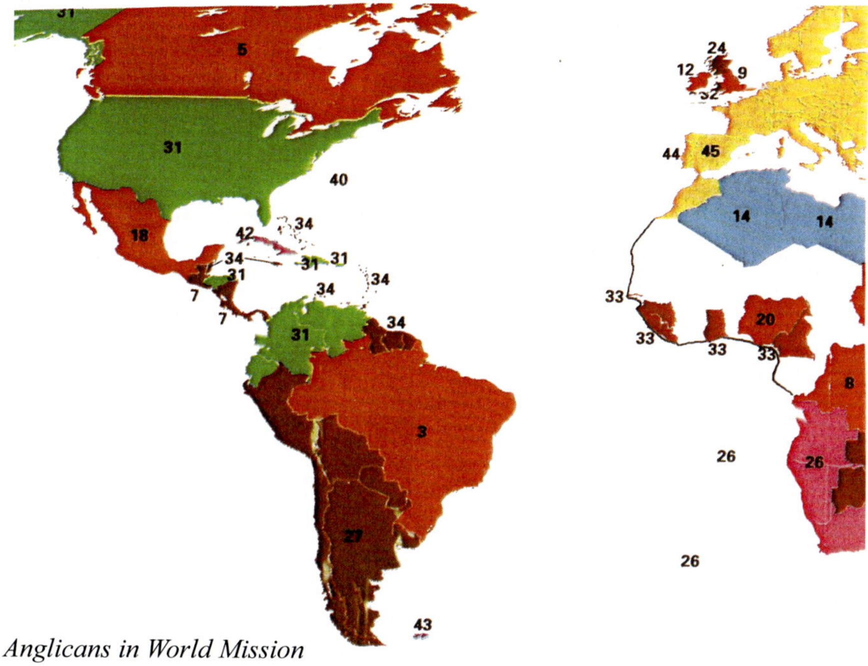

Anglicans in World Mission

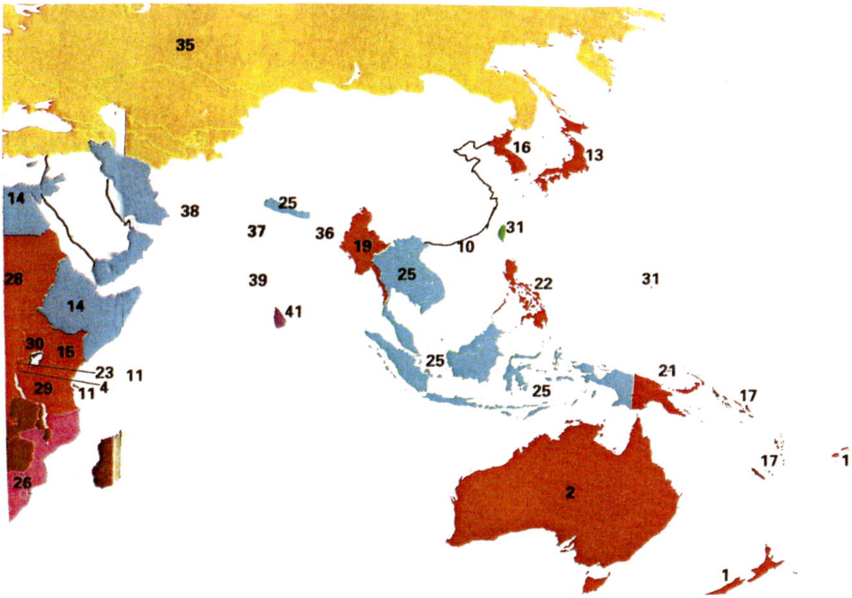

How to Have Beautiful Thoughts

The thought process is the key to the universe. It is communication between likeminded thoughts. The brain is a powerhouse for transmitting thoughts. The thought process travels in the spiritual plane at vast speeds outside of known scientific laws, and meets other thoughts in the universe. Now you can see why we must send out lovely thoughts. Imagine you drop a stone in the water from the middle of a pond. The waves travel to the side of the pond and rebound with added strength to the position where the stone was dropped in. If you send out negative bad vibe thoughts, like the waves on the pond that rebound with added strength, you will one day receive back your negative thoughts with added weight.

There are rules for producing the best thoughts and with the strongest transmissions. The ability to concentrate is paramount.

1) To focus on events. In your mind you must build up the complete picture to transmit.

2) What actions do you want to take in building up this picture?

3) Are these actions the right ones to achieve your goal? What are the consequences likely to result from these actions?

4) If you are satisfied the picture and desire to achieve is strong, send the thought transmissions on positive strength and knowledge it will be achieved.

To assist you in your judgment consider the following:

1) Are you the best judge between what is desirable and what is undesirable?

2) Examine your own behaviour especially your mental attitude to generate peacefulness. Emotions can be positive and negative.

Two desires may assist your judgment:

1) One is the aspiration to be a benefit to all.

2) The other is the aspiration to attain fully the enlightened state for that purpose.

If you wish to transmit love and happiness this would benefit any receivers of your transmission. You can only transmit this if you have happiness and love in your heart. The sense of contentment is a key factor for attaining happiness. Later I discuss the benefits from an understanding of Hindu thinking and Buddhism in reasoning and developing the thought process, as well as the part meditation plays.

Jesus' Sayings

1) 'I do not speak My own authority but the Father who dwells in Me does the work.'

2) 'If you can believe, all things are possible to him who believes.'

3) 'Therefore I say to you, whatever things you ask when you pray believe that you receive them and you will have them.'

4) His disciples were unable to cast out a demon. They asked Jesus, 'Why could we not cast it out?' Jesus replied 'Because of your unbelief.'

The Meanings of Words

The Bible is full of mistakes. This is the result of language translations. In our language we sometimes do not have enough words to express our feelings. The English language is typical of this problem.

Translating our thoughts into another language can create a different meaning. In some languages there are no similar words to express ourselves. An adjective may alter the meaning of a noun. An infinite number of variations may follow.

Imagine a beautiful orange. Your orange may be smaller than mine. My orange has scent and fragrance. My orange is a different colour to yours. For all the differences we still recognise it as a beautiful orange. An artist may paint many different oranges. The written word is not the only way of expression. I could have a thought which I cannot express in words.

We were all made from energy. If we lived in a world of energy only, we could have a way of recognising each other by recognising the type of characteristics of that energy. A thought could be expressed as an abstract shape, a painting, a moving energy form. I could ask that thought form to show your true identity. Mind is energy to communicate with other minds.

The Greeks have four words for the meaning of love –

1)	agape	pure love in reference to God
2)	phileo	the love of friendship
3)	storge	the love of a parent
4)	eros	in romantic love, involving commitment

How would I categorise the following?

1) I love your hairstyle.

2) I love the smell of your cooking.

Perhaps I should use different words - Your hairstyle is very beautiful. The smell of your cooking makes me dribble out of the corner of my mouth.

Words used by Jesus 2000 years ago may have a slightly different meaning today. Perhaps not if we trace the Greek words used. Miracles were defined as 'workings of powers' from the Greek word dunamis – which also means mighty deeds. In the Bible God reveals to us that if we continue to cast out evil spirits miraculous healings will follow, which translated from the Greek means mighty deeds and workings of powers.

In Derek Prince's book *The Gifts of the Spirit* he says;

'I have learned the crucial point in a miracle is getting a person to do a small act that starts his faith moving.'

Jesus said in Matthew 9.29, 'according to your faith be it unto you.' Most people don't believe things unless they can see them. It is from our senses against our stored memory patterns we arrive at conclusions. Whether we act on our conclusions is a different story.

From the chapter on the human brain we know our brains are accessible. A thought can be put into our head, an answer to a question you put to Jesus. You may prefer it if I say your brain can receive a thought.

In Corinthians 12.28 we read, 'and God has appointed these in the church: first apostles, second prophets, third teachers and after that miracles, then gifts of healing.'

So perhaps some of us are chosen by God for a purpose, and we know God can work through the cells in our brain which receive the Divine Mind. Corinthians 12.10 says 'to one is given a gift, to another a different gift and to another is given prophecy.' Prophecy is an important act in the Bible, that knowledge is given that will come true in the future. So much knowledge was given in Hebrew and Aramaic. In translations from the Hebrew we can have more than one interpretation, or perhaps a different message.

Jesus called the Holy Spirit the comforter. In Greek a similar translation is parakletos which means 'one called in alongside you'. Do I know it!

When I thought I was dying in pain in December 2005 on my sailing yacht moored alongside Grenada Yacht Club I came back from shopping at midday, opened up the hatch to go below, and the outline shape of Jesus was on the starboard bunk with a massive Holy Presence, which lasted 2 weeks. Jesus came to comfort me, not to heal me; that happened 9 months later on 21st September 2006.

Paul wrote 'Blessed be the God and Father of our Lord Jesus Christ, the Father of mercies and God of all comfort. God is the God of all comfort.' 2 Corinthians 1.3

My scientific friends want to see proof of religion in scientific terms.

We don't have the science at present, but we will in the future. I say to them, if you want to work with chemical reactions you need chemicals in a test tube and once the reaction between different substances start to work to create change, you observe the result and reproducing the experiment get the same result. If you want to work with gasses you need a test tube of gasses. There are rules for working and analysing the atom smasher in the Cern Tunnel in Switzerland, in terms of particles, energy and quantum physics.

I say to them if you wish to experiment in my field you need a test tube of love and belief in God. Then add your chemicals and analyse the result. Can you see into the spirit world? I know some people who can. Once you believe that Jesus Christ is the Son of God you are in the scientific medium in which miracles, healings and a Divine Understanding takes place. The active ingredient in the experiment is the Divine Spirit of God which permeates everything.

Teaching the piano at St Mary's Anglican church Bequia

A Vision

I saw a picture in my imagination that could hang from the cross beam in St Mary's church. When I drew the picture I realised I had drawn the Island of Bequia in the background. I gave the picture to an artist to paint, as seen here.

Jesus in the Caribbean

Chapter Six

Creation from the Divine Principle Downwards

Out of darkness there came a Divine white light tinged with flames of gold. This was the Divine Principle and God, the Light of the World. Music came with the Divine Principle. This was recorded in the translation of the Old Babylonian tablets in the Taw Cross Temple. Jesus tells us he lives in the Celestial Realm with other Grand Masters. Many mediums have agreed with my ladder, including Indians who have left their physical bodies and gone in spirit to meet relatives in India. Some astral voyages have been written about in detail, and many energy and forms on Dimension Four have been described. Baird Spalding's stories tell of the teaching on Dimension Six and great insight into the spiritual world and how everything is represented in energy by a different means.

On 12th June 2008 I went to a lecture by Divaldo Franco. This remarkable man, now aged 80, has spent his whole life raising money for poor people and children in Brazil and teaching and caring for the sick. As a child he played with children from the next dimension. He can clearly see beyond the grave. He supported my Dimension Six, sending people to all corners of the universe to teach. In Baird Spalding's book Jesus took eleven scientists over the garden fence to see the next life. Everything carries on the same. The eleven scientists in the same year, 1895, spent 4 months translating the copies of the Old Babylonian tablets in the Taw Cross Temple with the help of translators. This gives the story of the coming of the Divine White Light and names God in Spirit. Also there are writings from the Taw Cross Temple in Tibet which are copies of the Old Babylonian tablets from 45,000 BC, and writings from the Vedas, which gives a history of creation when God was named in spirit.

This is printed below:

'The 'Lord God' was used to designate the Perfect Being that the Divine Principles, or God, created to bring out His qualities here on earth. This Being was created in the image and likeness of the Divine Principle and had access to, and could use, everything that the Divine Principle had. This Being was given power and dominion over every condition that existed upon the earth. This Being had all the potentialities of the Divine Principle and the power to bring them forth as long as He co-operated with the Divine Principle and developed the faculties that have been given Him, in the ideal way that the Divine Principle had planned or was holding in mind. This Being was afterwards called 'Lord God', which meant expression in creative action or the Law of God. This is the Perfect Being that the Divine Principle holds in mind for man to express. This is the Divine and Only Man that the Divine Principle created. Man, or the spiritual side of his nature, has access to and can become this Lord God or One Man. This Divine Man afterwards became known as the Christ. He had dominion over heaven and earth and all things therein. Then the Lord God, using His power to create, did create other beings like unto Himself. These beings were afterwards called sons of the Lord God and their Creator was called Father and the Divine Principle was called God.'

I saw the door to heaven open and God was writing a message. 'WANTED – good teachers for overseas postings.'

Creation

Divine Principle (with the laws of science & universal substance)

Divine White Light

Two greatest words are God & Love	Created Lord God ↓	(to govern planet earth Jesus said 'In God's house there are many rooms or dimensions')
A U M	love, love, music	

Dimension Seven (The celestial realm)

Where all there greatest prophets and masters guide the destiny of the world (Osiris, Buddha, Jesus)

Divine white light

↙ ↓ ↘

Music love love music

Dimension Six

Great scientists, leaders. Artists, musicians, doctors, philosophers, spiritualists, sending their services to all corners of the universe

Divine white light

↙ ↓ ↘

Music love love music

Dimension Five (barrier layer)

Angels of beauty, coloured lights, choirs of heaven.

Divine white light

↙ ↓ ↘

Music love love music

Dimension Four

Every living thought, form energy. Matter, a thought can create a form you can challenge the form for its true identity.

Divine white light

↙ ↓ ↘

Music love love music

You can contact dimension four to see the product of creation. Lower energy forms exist

Dimension Three

Divine white light

↙ ↓ ↘

One and a half million years ago two miracles started and were completed 250,000 years ago; mans voice box was constructed and the human brain became three times as large, enabling syntax, the construction of sentences for recall and communication. God in his love, wanted to share the beauty and diversity of creation so man could reach God within himself. With knowledge and wisdom and positive thought to transmit love and peace.

Dimension Two

Divine white light

↙ ↓ ↘

Every living creature on Earth unable to produce sentences for storage and recall but still able to communicate by instinct and contact with others and the environment.

Chapter Seven

Climbing the ladder to God – meditation

To God within

Love, peace purity, perfection, truth, visualisation of the perfect form.
The seed is planted. The flower is perfect.

Leave all earthly values behind which are lower energies.

Learn how Jesus did all the miracles.

Projecting the clear image to be achieved and with complete understanding of universal laws which cannot be changed and in full confidence projecting it.

God Mind (Christ of God presence)

Music – love

'When two or more are gathered together all spiritual together in my name to teaching to pass of

Myself I can do nothing and it is God within me that does the work.'

Much learning and study of all spiritual energies and devotion on knowledge. Only with wisdom and understanding can the God mind be reached.

Christ conscious or Buddha attainment

Living in the Christ consciousness

Living the perfect life of love, positive thinking, good deeds, compassion and peace. An example to all.

Conscious Mind

Conscious Mind

The senses produce consciousness	↑ The Chakra wheel turns upwards. Motor side of Brain sends out response.

Intelligent man with vocal chords to make speech, and a large brain for syntax. The human brain was completed250,000 years ago to attain wisdom by learning. The human brain alters it's circulatory and adapts as time goes by a computer does not.

The word God when spoken carries the highest vibrational frequency.

The word love when spoken carries the second highest vibrational frequency. God in Hindu is AUM.

Climbing the Ladder to God Within

You need knowledge, divine understand, love and charity, purity, perfection, belief and desire to create. You need to understand healing and creating peace and to know Jesus is the Son of God. You must understand your Divine Inheritance.

Start by reading *Need to Know* Christianity from its ancient roots to its modern relevance by Peter Graystone, published by Collins ISBN 978-0.00-7261161.

Man is good because he is the offspring of God, He must stay in harmony with the Universal

Principle. Everything must be turned round for the good, in-harmony must become harmony.

There can be no discord. Music is an important part of Divine Spirit for it carries harmony and healing.

The individual must learn to understand Universal Law. Peace and happiness have to be earned by your sincere efforts.

You must understand and love the Law of God. Jesus says, 'I live in spirit.' There is no such thing as time and space in spirit. Spirit doesn't consider evil, poverty or disease. In higher planes of spiritual existence these things do not exist, pain and suffering exist on Earthly planes.

To reach purity you need to give up all negative words and never say them again. Anger, hatred, jealousy, revenge, wishing pain on anyone; all these things must be removed from your thought, and in its place remember to 'love thy enemies.' Read the Sermon on the Mount. We can purify the mind with meditation. Let the love of music flow through you, and learn to be at peace within yourself. Then we can show our lives as an example to all. Learn to be content with what you've got. Mental calmness is a very important factor for good health. The more you show concern about the welfare and rights of others, the more you are a genuine friend.

Karuna is infinite compassion and kindness.

Friends will come and help you in time of trouble. The four noble truths state:

1) There is suffering
2) Suffering has cause
3) There is cessation of suffering
4) There is a path to such freedom

Pain and suffering will need to be isolated and dealt with. Every effort must be made to cure pain as soon as possible. The universal law of cause and effect means you must heal the cause to eliminate the effect.

Understanding

God made the perfect child, the child, from which we are all descended. By inheritance we are all Divine. As the mighty oak tree shows new buds as perfect as the first ones it produced 100 years before, so every child born is another perfect child of the Christ.

Energy Levels

Sir Jagadish Chandra Bose of Calcutta University spent his life in research and developing knowledge in the field of energy patterns. He discovered microwaves and contributed to nuclear research and the atom bomb.

Plants have an energy level that stays with them for life.

Animals have a higher energy level that stays with them for life.

Humans have the highest energy level that stays with them for life.

The word GOD carries the highest vibrational level. The word LOVE carries the second highest vibrational energy level. He quotes a figure for the power of thought transmission as 20,000 times the speed of light which travels in a different medium.

The word GOD in Hindu is AUM (pronounced OM) and is the most sacred word in India and Tibet. It is chanted by thousands of people going on religious pilgrimages, so the rocks at Pora Tat Sang Monastery vibrate with the spoken word AUM.

The energy levels from the top of our head, the crown chakra, can be raised to communicate with the celestial realm.

Devotion and commitment to leading the perfect life in Jesus' teachings together with meditations of love will help us up the ladder to reach to the first stage, the Christ Consciousness or Buddha Attainment. This means we need to draw up a plan of daily worship and check we stick to our goal to achieve.

Meditation on Love

I went to Holland and there I saw a field of red flowers. They are the red blossoms of the clover plant, which stand about twelve inches above the ground. Then I saw a little girl walk across the field on top of the red clover flowers to the other side of the field. She is returned toward me.

I said to her, 'Your feet never touched the ground; how did you do it?'

'I don't know.' said the little girl, 'but I love the little red clover flowers and they love me so much that when I walk across the field they hold my feet up in the air.'

The Next Rung up the Ladder is The God Mind (Christ of God

Presence).

Jesus said, 'Love your enemies.' How easy is it to hate your enemies and bear a grudge against them? Meditation can help you to understand the need for peace of mind for your own health. The Buddhist meditation of equalisation and equanimity asks you to reflect on your attitude to friends and enemies and the effect they have on your peace of mind. What are your thoughts when you are with a group of good friends, a group of disinterested individuals, a group of enemies? How do they view your attitude toward them? Ask yourself, on what grounds do you discriminate between people? Concentrate on the equality between yourself and all other beings. Not only do you have to generate peace and contentment in your own mind, you have to generate peace in the minds of others.

Divine Understanding

Divine understanding is the Will of God. Jesus tells us the Will of God in His teachings which we must obey. Praise and love God for the beauty of creation, the beauty of flowers, the love of nature. Treat animals with kindness and the understanding they deserve. If you love them they will not be afraid of you. The Divine Spirit permeates everything, so we need to draw it into ourselves to operate with God inside us. We are all descended from the perfect child, The Christ, so by hereditary we are all Divine. We have cells in our brain that receive messages from the Divine Mind. If we activate God from within everything else follows. Divine understanding is knowledge and wisdom. Think of a notice in heaven – 'God wants good teachers' – are you a good teacher? Can you apply for the job?

Next you have to understand life in the spiritual world. There is no time, no space barriers and you travel in your spiritual body which can be projected in several places at once. Your thought process carries spiritual form. Jesus said we live in the celestial realm, you call it seventh heaven, in the invisible to you, but visible to ourselves. It is the ability to project the clear image to be achieved for good purposes in the knowledge of Universal Laws.

An understanding of your spiritual body on earth is very important.

Seven chakras down your head and body are connected to another 42 or more chakras, one in each hand, one in each foot etc. These moving energy wheels can be photographed on Kirlian photography. The spiritual body can never be destroyed, and lifts off at death of the physical body. It interacts with the physical body through the etheric aura which is close to the body and these auras are shown on Kirlian photography. Continuous photography of these auras show an ever changing interaction which is influenced by thought and mental wellbeing. All the chakras are connected together by thousands of kundali lines of power and connect to the brain. Disease and malfunction of the body show up in these chakras first, before the physical body, and shows how important our spiritual wellbeing is to our physical body.

Your spiritual body never dies. It cannot be destroyed. If you lose a limb you can feel the limb still present in the etheric aura. Pain and suffering do not exist in the spiritual world. If you live close to God in this life there is no such thing as death, as you ride over it. Your soul (spirit is the same thing) leaves the body. Sir Chandra Bose at Calcutta University has photographed it leaving the body many times. The etheric aura is the connection between the spiritual and physical bodies and contains the mould for the new body and the brain memory patterns accompany it to form a new body in one to three days. In the next life you have to abide by universal laws which cannot be changed. In the Divine picture, if progress diverges too far from the desired path, cosmic laws bring it back into line.

We can be with Jesus in spirit, which is our soul contact. We can talk to Jesus and He will answer by direct replies to our brain. Sometimes Jesus comes to you and you can see His outline in spiritual shape. In the journeys with the Masters of the Far East, Jesus and many of the Grand Masters appeared in their own bodies.

Let me take you on a spiritual journey in meditation.

In this meditation I am sitting in a garden of flowers in summertime, a warm sunny day with only a little breeze. The sky is blue above, the grass is green and soft below. Every flower is in bloom from red roses, yellow ones, white and pink carnations, and many others. God's Divine white light enters every flower and breaks into the seven colours of the rainbow, so that each colour is radiating healing properties, and their perfumes add a radiance that transports you into the spiritual world. There is a great feeling of peace and tranquility on this garden. I think I will lie down on the green grass and put a pillow under my head. I can hear the distant sound of music like a choir singing a Puccini opera drifting across the fields.

Just then, Jesus walks into the garden and says, 'Let's go for a walk together down by the sea shore.'

We set off for a windy path through tall trees and reeds and the grass gave way to sand as we reached the beach. The waves are breaking on the shore, but on the other side of the bay we could see a wooden pier extending out in the water.

'Let's walk together to the pier and walk out on the end to watch the reflections in the water.'

In the distance I can see splashing in the water, like a lot of big fish having fun. They are dolphins and they are coming this way, jumping higher and higher as they approach us. There are six of them. The displays they are creating are all for our benefit. They want to make us happy. Jesus and I don't want to leave but it is getting late and time to go home. Our feet hardly seem to touch the ground as we skip along the beach to the other side of the bay and find the path up to the house. As we approach the garden I look so peaceful asleep on the grass. I say goodbye to Jesus and thank you for coming on the walk. Now I must join my physical body and together we go into the house for a cup of tea.

This is another meditation which I call My Meditation to God.

I am going to take David Fontana's book to read in the garden *The Elements of Meditation*, ISBN 186204036-2.

I go into the garden on another lovely summer's day with all my flowers displaying every beautiful colour, just to relax. I find a relaxing chair and start reading David Fontana's book on the elements of meditation. The benefits of meditation are emotional release and generating feelings of peace and independence. I put the book down to look again around my garden, the layout of flowers, shrubs and trees.

Everything in the garden is in harmony. I believe they are all in love with one another creating a golden pattern in God's creation.

The trees are beckoning me to visit them. In the corner of the garden is a tree with its branches extending outwards from every side. Now I stand in front of the tree and raise my arms at right angles to my body like the branches of the tree. I turn the palms of my hands upwards towards the sky and look upwards into the top of the tree and look beyond into the blue sky and see God standing in the sky with his arms outstretched pouring love down to every corner of the earth. Please God pour your love into our heart so we can go forth and tell everyone there is only one god.

I ask you to read two further books:

1) The Illustrated *Book of Sacred Scriptures* by Timothy Freke ISBN 0722535682

2) All six volumes of *Life and Teaching of the Masters of the Far East* by Baird T Spalding – De Vorss and Co Publishers, PO Box 1389, Camarillo, CA 930111 – 1389. ISBN 0875165389.

The Illustrated Book of Sacred Scriptures

Never before have so many of the World's sacred writings been available to English speaking readers. It invites readers to discover for themselves the perennial wisdom that lies at the heart of humanity's rich spiritual heritage. Each subject is discussed in the light of many different religions to arrive at conclusions givin.g a comprehensive approach to that subject. It concludes that *there is only one God.*

Objects associated with prayer

1 Icon (religious painting) of Christ or Mary (Orthodox)

2 Crucifix; Statuette of Christ crucified on a cross

3 Rosary beads (one for each prayer) with crucifix and Mary medallion (Roman Catholic)

There are Moral Laws and Universal Laws

Moral Laws apply to everyday living and are:

1) Laws of Nature
2) Law of Preservation
3) Law of Reproduction
4) Law of Destruction
5) Law of Work and Labour
6) Law of Society (requires of you)
7) Law of Progress and Moral Perfection
8) Law of Equality
9) Law of Love and Charity and Justice
10) Law of Liberty (free speech and thinking)
11) Law of Worship

There are universal laws that apply to all worlds. Without a knowledge of these you cannot do Divine Spiritual healing e.g. The Law of Cause and Effect.

Universal laws

(there are other ones)

Just as there are physical laws like gravity and relativity that govern the physical world, there are laws which govern the mental world we create in. In all existence there is structure, order and form. This is true in the realm of creativity as well as people who accomplish their ideals are co-operating with the Universal Laws whether they know it or not because the truth always prevails.

1) Believing and knowing encapsulates the essence of creative imagery. A belief occurs when you have completely imaged something. The key to using the Law of Believing and Knowing, therefore, is to create a complete, detailed thought-form image and act upon it until your

desired thought is manifested into physical reality. With practice you will discover that your thoughts are things and you will discover the reality or mind substance. Belief creates more belief, for the more you practice imagining first following it with activity, the more you will know how to reproduce success in your life.

2) The Law of Abundance provides the means for you to receive into your life more than you have at the present. He who aids others to abundance will always have abundance. This is an infallible law.

3) The Law of Proper Perspective means determining what is most important to you and what will produce soul growth. Learn how to put things first! Write down daily everything that you want and need to accomplish.

4) Law of Cause and Effect, thought is cause, and the effect is its manifest likeness. You create your reality with thought, your subconscious mind can only reproduce what your conscious mind creates. Therefore, what you experience in your life is the effect (results) of your thinking. Putting this law into practice will give you a way to understand true responsibility. The first responsibility you have is to your Self – to respond to the desires of your soul. Your soul craves maturity. Fill your soul with understandings of creation.

5) The Law of Attraction dictates that like attracts like. When your thought-form has been planted, it reaches out with thought waves to the entire universe. There is a universal mind in which all of our minds connect. There will always be other minds with desires and needs compatible to your own. These other minds are also creating visualized thought-forms which reach out into universal mind. When these similar thought-forms meet, the attraction produces a match.

6) The law of Ten Fold Return states that when you give freely, you can expect to receive ten times what you have given, enabling you to give ten times more. Visualization produces great success when coupled with the use of the Law of Ten Fold Return. When you give, you can always expect to receive.

Knowing that there are Universal Laws will help you in your use of visualization. When you practice creative imagery, you can draw upon power greater than your own. Forces unseen to your eyes and heard not by your ears are at work, ready to aid you to fulfill your desires. In the beginning, trust that these mysterious energies are available to you as you experiment you will become more familiar with their beneficence.

When You Create Only Do So for a Good Perfect Reason

Only transmit words of love and beauty. If you drop a stone in the water of a pond, waves will travel outwards to the side of the pond and rebound with strength to the point at which the stone entered the pond. Likewise, your thought transmission will travel outwards and will rebound and come back to you. Do you want to receive negative thoughts? Then don't send them out.

Climbing the Ladder to God Within

Jesus said that you can do as I can do and even greater things you can do. Now with all your knowledge you can ask Jesus to help you get God within. Remember – in any lesson when the attainment is reached, forget the lesson, remember the attainment. It is the thought in the top of our head which we must develop by spiritual thought. The highest vibrations are produced by the words GOD and LOVE. To raise your energy level to God within use words of adoration, thanking God for beautiful flowers, the knowledge of the absolute truth, perfection and purity for you to achieve.

Jesus also said, 'If you have faith I can show you how to contact God within you.' He said when the heavens were opened unto Him, He saw the law of expression, whereby ideas conceived in the Divine mind are made into form. All forms may be transformed or changed in form though a change of consciousness in regard to it. Every good desire man has is God's desire. There is an unlimited supply in the universal God substance everywhere about us to meet every desire.

It is stated in the Gospels that, 'All things are possible to them that believe.' Allow the universal mind to flow into your personal mind, and you will be building the temple of the living God within you. Then the Holy Spirit fills the consciousness.

The power of the brain to transmit positive thought is unlimited. When you create it must be for the benefit of mankind and only positive thoughts. You must raise your consciousness to the Christ consciousness, and then through the God mind, access the highest and most sacred level, the Divine Mind. Heaven is a perfect state of consciousness, a wonderful God-given spiritual world. The world is full of creation, the beauty and diversity of creation, which God has made for us, his children to enjoy. Man must practice sending positive thoughts of love, harmony, peace and perfection. We do not have the Divine Mind, but we do have access to the Divine Mind.

Chapter Eight

The Spiritual Body – Chakras and Auras and the Human Energy Field

5000 years ago ancient spiritual tradition of India spoke of a universal source of all life. This energy they called Prana. Yogis work with the energy with the breathing techniques, meditation and physical exercises to produce altered states of consciousness and longevity.

3000 years ago the Ancient Qigong Masters in China were practicing their meditation discipline to balance and invigorate the Human Energy Field, called QI. Gong means working with QI. When QI is balanced, the entity has good health, unbalanced bad health.

538 BC. The Kabbalah, Jewish Mystical Teachers called these energies the astral light. Paintings showed auras around the heads of Priests, Buddha and Jesus (halo). More is known of the aura today.

Diagnosis of illness may be seen in auras and chakras. Mediums and scientists have to work together as we have a science which behaves outside normal scientific understanding.

The Universal Energy or Divine Spirit does exist in everything and there is an abundance of universal laws governing everything, which must be obeyed. We can use Divine Spirit for healing. Many different things can contribute toward healing, love being very important.

The human energy fields around our bodies are numerous and complicated. Thermal air currents are continuous and constantly changing with the body radiating heat and reflecting heat in different parts of the body at different times. Electro magnetic fields are numerous and change under the influence of the interaction between the spiritual body, the etheric aura and the physical body. The kundalini lines relay messages to the brain from every part of the body. You can photograph the aura and see the ever changing colours produced by the aura. This is linked to your ever changing emotions and physical wellbeing. It follows that patterns produced could lead to diagnostic conclusions about your spiritual and physical bodies.

The spiritual body consists of chakras of which there are seven from the top of the head to the base of the spine, one in each hand and foot and about 45 in different parts of the body. The seven main ones correspond to the seven main nerve ganglia in the spinal cord. Chakras are revolving energy centres of electro magnetic energy which can be photographed with high energy photography called Kirlian photography. Their existence has been known since 2000 BC and described by the Aryans. The word in Sanskrit means wheel and refers to the chariot wheels of the invading Aryans. The correct spelling is cakra. Also the word denotes the wheel of time, kalacakra, and the sun carrying the ruler of all time around the world in a triumphant chariot called cakra a'vartin. The wheel appears on the Indian National Flag.

The chakras display colours from the base upwards - red, orange, yellow, green, blue, purple and white light. If a person lies down you can trace the chakras using a quartz crystal as a pendulum. Hold the pendulum over each chakra area and watch the pendulum turn, first anticlockwise and then clockwise.

It is estimated that there are 30,000 kundalini lines of force directing lines of force to every cell of the body and the brain. In Baird Spalding's books it is described as producing the vitality of the life fluid. The chakras can be located also by divining rods. Surrounding the body, and close to it, is the etheric aura which acts like a blueprint or mould of the body. This is the interaction layer between the spiritual body and physical body.

The chakras need to be well energized for you to be in good health. The chakras need to be well balanced with their neighbour. Under energized can lead to physical illness, good energy to wholeness of mind, body and spirit. The highest chakras at the top of the head relate to our mental state and connections to the spiritual, the chakras at the lower part of our body are related to physical needs.

Some Chakra Characteristics

Crown chakra	white/purple	connections to divine spiritual energy
Brow chakra	indigo	processes psychic and intuitive awareness
Throat chakra	blue	spiritual and psychic connection/capabilities
Heart chakra	green	promotes love, compassion, understanding
Solar plexus chakra	yellow	power, authority, love of learning
Sacral chakra	orange	creativity, sexual energy, emotions
Base chakra	red	survival, courage, vitality-ground to earth dissolves negativity

From the Kirlian photos you can see the 7 coloured chakra centres and the ever changing colours of the auras. Rainbow auras give you a 22 page print out of all the meanings of your auras and energy levels.

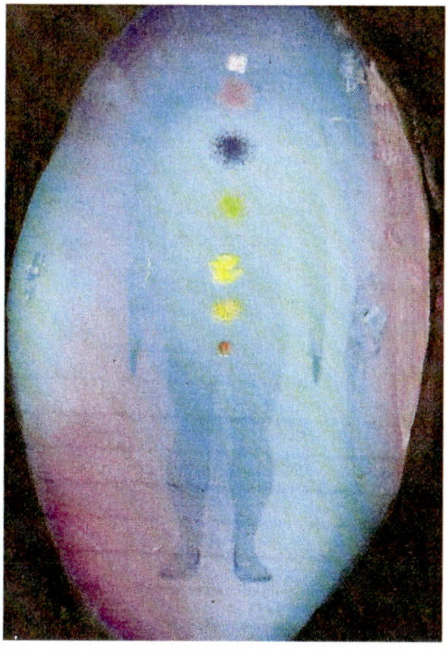

Your Aura Colours:

Deep Red:	realistic, grounded, active, survival-oriented
Red:	active, powerful, energetic, vitality, competitive, winner, strong willpower sexual, passionate, relates to the physical body
Orange-Red:	artistic, physical-creative expression, confidence, creative power, excitement
Orange:	creative, productive, adventurous, courageous, relates to emotions
Orange-Yellow:	analytical thinker, creative, intelligent, scientific, detail oriented, perfectionist
Yellow:	creative, intelligent, playful, lightness, optimistic, easy-going, relates to life energy
Yellow-Green:	communicative, logical, balanced, creative with heart
Green:	teacher, social communicator, love people, animals, nature
Blue-Green:	healer, therapist, sensitive, peace, tranquility, compassionate
Blue:	caring, sensitive, loving, helpful, intuition, love to help others
Indigo:	intuitive, sensitive, loyal, deep feelings, relates to the third eye, visual
Violet:	intuitive, artistic, magical, futuristic, idealistic, relates to the crown
Lavender:	imagination, visionary, daydreamer, etheric
White:	spiritual transcendent, higher dimensions, etheric, non-physical qualities

How Can We Energise the Chakras?

1) Spiritual energy is when we channel the body with our hands to bring divine spiritual energy into the body. If anyone asks 'what is spiritual energy?' tell them it is the Will of God.

We don't touch the person. You can feel the energy passing through our hands. The person's body starts feeling warm. Our hands become a diagnostic tool to feel under energized areas and breaks in the aura. We aim for chakra balancing and releasing blocked energy (granthi).

2) Crystal types to energise the individual chakras

The Crown Chakra – amethyst, clear quartz, diamond, selenite

The Third Eye Chakra – azurite tanzanite, sodalite, lapis lazuli

The Throat Chakra – blue lace agate, aquamarine, lapis lazuli, sodalite

The Heart Chakra – emerald, green jade, tourmaline, rose quartz, rhodocrosite

The Solar Plexus Chakra – citrine, turquoise, malachite, topaz

The Sacral Chakra – tigers eye, carnelian, firestone, red jasper

The Root Chakra – red garnet, ruby, black obsidian, bloodstone

3) Chakra meditations use mudras which are special hand positions to open chakras. The mudras have the power to send more energy to particular chakras. Sounds are chanted. A as in ah, and M is pronounced mng.

This can be found at:
http://www.electricenergies.com/chakras/open.php

When you open your chakras there are negative energies, which you must keep out. This is called grounding and protection. A natural way to ground is to be in the garden or doing some physical exercise. Ungrounded you may feel spacey, headachy, out of balance.

There are other ways. This chapter is not about how to be a healer. You must go on courses for spiritual healing.

The Aura

All people, animals and plants have auras. It is an ever changing pattern. Your Kirlian photograph another day would be different. It can reveal information about our physical, mental, emotion and spiritual wellbeing. It is as if God's divine energy is in touch with everything that is living by high electromagnetic energies.

Layer 1 – The Etheric Aura (appears on Kirlian photography)

Only an inch away from the body it follows its outline around the body. It can be 'felt' by spiritual healers who can detect a person's state of physical and mental health. An amputated limb can still be felt because its spiritual counterpart is still present. The etheric aura then is the connection or interplay between the spiritual and physical bodies.

Layer 2 – The Aura of the Emotions

This layer is about twelve inches from the body. It does not follow the body outline; it gives off the emotional state of mind.

Layer 3 – The Aura of Mind and Mental Process

This layer is about twenty inches away from the body and doesn't follow its outline. It contains all our thought processes. It is at a very high vibrational energy rate.

Layer 4 – The Aura of the Higher Mind and Spiritual Body

It can be some distance from the body. It is a spiritual aura, making the boundary between our spiritual being and our physical body. It is here we receive love and give out love and communicate with the divine light. The outer auras may be purple and brilliant blue, and can blend into white/silver. Gold on the soul level communicates with Divinity. This is our soul level.

Definition – ATMA = soul conversing with soul, using no other medium.

To find the boundary layer of an aura, come inwards with your hands until you feel a resistance. You can also feel the boundary areas with a pendulum. When you have understood and experienced the four levels of aura you reach soul level. This is where you connect to higher spiritual centres from the top of your head. It is only at these three soul levels true healing takes place.

Spiritual teachers of healing describe three higher spiritual places, where negative thoughts cannot exist and all earthly psychic forces are discarded. At the start of a spiritual healing course you are told you don't have to have a belief in God. This is for all to do. We don't do faith healing. You are told unless you reach soul level and contact with the highest spiritual energies, true healing will not take place.

There are 4 levels of healing at chakra and aura levels, and three higher levels of soul. The top level of soul contact leads you to your Golden Door, or words to the effect. Everything suggests to me they are making contact with high energy spirits. For me, I believe this level is when you get God inside you. Jesus said, 'Of myself I can do nothing. It is God inside of me that does everything. You can do as I can do.'

I was talking to a lady on a course, who wore a beautiful cross around her neck.

I asked 'Do you believe in Jesus.' 'No' she said, 'this is ornamental, it's the fashion.'

The teachers of spiritual healing refer to spiritual energy, the highest level to reach out to in healing, but don't call it God. Why? Because when they advertise their courses saying you don't have to believe in God to do spiritual healing it leaves the door open for those that don't believe to join the course. If the people joining the course turn out to have mediumship qualities that can be developed; there is a connection to the Fourth Dimension for healing where spiritual doctors can give advice to mediums. Take the example set by Betty Shine and the incredible contact she had with doctors from the next life.

Spiritual healing centres offer love, help and comfort. They give reassurance to cancer patients and the dying. If you question them about their healing capabilities they say everyone benefits to a lesser extent. If you ask them how many blind people have you restored sight to, how many cancer patients have they cured, I expect the answer will be none. They say this is not faith healing.

Mediums use their ability to look deeper into these questions we ask. They divide the five senses to use each one to greater ability. Also we must raise our brain vibrational energy rate to reach greater awareness. We must accept the ability to feel greater awareness, likewise to hear, to see spirit forms, the spiritual sense of smell and taste to give them names, their own individuality and train to use them.

Clairvoyance is the ability to see spirit in all forms, to hear voice, to feel, touch or even sense, to get the sense of taste, to sense smell. Clairaudience is the ability to hear voices. Clairentience is the ability to touch, feel or even sense. Clairoralience is the ability to get the taste. Clairalience is the ability to sense smell.

The lower chakras are for earthing, the highest chakras are for more spiritual matters.

I think a lot of psychic help comes from the Fourth Dimension from spiritual doctors trying to help the spiritual body. Clairvoyance is a medium's remarkable gift and can be very conclusive at times. Often this gift runs in families, the ability to use additional information from the electro-magnetic spectrum, the ability to communicate with the next dimension especially in the world of healing.

Many names come to mind, Harry Edwards a great spiritual distance healer and recently Betty Shine. Her books are a priority to read. Her first book called Mind to Mind published in 1989, originally published in Great Britain by Bantam Press, a Corgi book 0552135787. I quote from writings about her. Her extraordinary gifts, a clairvoyant ability to diagnose medically, her healing powers and her discovery of mind energy have made her one of Britain foremost healers.

Her next book was Mind Magic, a self-help guide that will enable everyone to experience the benefits of mind energy and healing for themselves and for the good of others. Another book is called The Infinite Mind.

Scientists always make the same mistakes; they fail to distinguish between the physical grey matter, the brain and the wonder of life itself, the mind. The Infinite Mind presents the proof for the existence of the mind independent of the biological functions of the brain.

Flowers have auras. Every living thing has an aura. It would be interesting to do a study to find the common denominator between different flower auras. My belief is in the divine white light that enters the crown chakra, enters the flowers and enters everything that is living. It brings with it the vibrational energy level or code for that thing and it stays with it for life. This was brought home to me when I went to a spiritual healer and a great white light flashed inside my head. This light has been photographed on Kirlian photography.

Divaldo Franco told us at a lecture he was doing spiritual healing work on epileptics and working with a team of neurologists working on brain studies, when the scientists saw a small white light at the top of the brain, the crown chakra. This white light breaks into seven colours of the rainbow, the colours my quartz crystals reveal from the sunlight, the colours of the seven chakras, the colours of flowers etc.

Energy levels were described by Sir Jagadish Chandra Bose at the Bose Institute (University) Calcutta. He said plants, flowers, nature have one energy level given to them, animals a higher one and humans the highest energy vibration levels.

In the Kirlain report by Rainbow auras@aol.com a 22 page handout on your chakra, aura balance is given to you.

1) Yin-yang balance (needles close together) indicates male-female energies seem to be in harmony.

2) Your mind-body-spirit graph gives you an overview of how your energies are distributed between body, mind and spirit.

3) Your emotional meter shows your emotional reaction, true thought and inner feelings.

4) Your state of mind-body graph displays your overall mind-body condition and is based on your body temperature i.e. Stress/relaxation graph.

5) Your energy levels graph is based on your electro-desmal activity. Unevenness in your chakra shows there is disharmony in your energy flow. Values given indicate your vibrational rate.

Also there are several pages on your aura colour analysis. Mine displays a lot of blue, with purple coming in, indigo blue over the head and green around the face. Green is associated with a teacher, social, communicator, love people, animals and nature.

The Heart Chakra

Divine love flows from the heart. Jesus said, 'Blessed are the pure in heart for they shall see God'. I am writing in more detail about this chakra which is called the Anahata chakra. Its colour is green or pink. To increase its energy use one of the following:

1) Sound – in toning use AH to the note F – which can be used together with mudras hand shapes.

2) Crystals giving healing energy – green jade, aventurine, rose quartz, watermelon, tourmaline, rhodocrosite.

3) Aromatherapy oils for healing – rose, bergamot, Melissa.

The heart chakra is located at the heart centre. There as a minor heart chakra which contains the Celestial Wishing Tree or Kalpataru, called the Anandakandu lotus (a kind of lily). It reminds me of our Christmas tree, brightly decorated, with the angel at the top and all our presents of love to each other at the bottom. The tree of life is mentioned in the Kabbalalistic beliefs, a study and belief in the ancient mysteries of the Bible. The Kabbalistic tree of life is a map of the paths of the Netherworld and the middle pillar relates directly to the chakras along our own middle pillar, the spine. By certain exercises involving the chakras and the snakelike kundalini energy it seems that the astral body can be perfected or transformed into a vehicle with a much longer lifespan. Some Egyptian papyri display the Wishing Tree as administrating 'spiritual nourishment' combining the concept of the world tree, tree of life and tree of knowledge.

The heart chakra is midway between the higher centres of psychic and higher spiritual centres and lower chakra centres controlling bodily functions and power. The heart chakra relates to the Star of David, with gentleness, compassion, acceptance, giving, divine love.

When in balanced energy it displays:

Friendliness, outgoing, active in the community, in touch with everyone's feelings, divine love and using the arms and hands we use to touch and hold the ones we love.

Sexuality - Can surrender and merge in a loving relationship, desires closeness of the body, mind and soul.

When not in balanced energy it displays:

Self doubt, over critical, tense between shoulder blades, possessive, moody, manic depressive.

Sexuality - Terrified of rejection, needs constant reassurance.

Physically - It is responsible for the heart, lungs, breast, immune system, thymus and lymph glands.

The Crown Chakra

Teachers of spiritual healing say healing occurs by channelling spiritual energy using your hands to energise and balance the chakras, to find under energized areas which need more channeling, and to feel the aura boundaries and areas of blocked energy. You need to study the 7 main chakras. There are different words used to describe the chakras depending on which books you read. For example in Ashtanga yoga the crown chakra is called Sahasrara chakra and this is its description: It is located at the crown of your head and is known as the thousand-petalled lotus. It is the final destination of cosmic energy. Another definition which is generally accepted is that this is our direct link with the source and the gateway for spiritual light.

My definition is: Divine spiritual energy is the will of God and connects through the crown chakra as a divine white light for healing.

If you are very religious and believe in Jesus, the thought must have entered your head – I wish I could heal people like Jesus does. This is faith healing. If you wish to do a course on spiritual healing contact your nearest centre. I recommend you read a book Spiritual Healing, a practical guide to hands on healing by Jack Angelo ISBN 184181-149-1.

The Beauty and Diversity of Creation

The Kabbalah and the Celestial Wishing Tree - Kalpataru

The Kabbalah and the Torah are from 3,400 years ago. They were written when God spoke to Moses, and the first five books of the Bible, OnKelos, indicate that the real divine gift is the ability to form the sounds of speech and to use language to forge a relationship with God. The enlargement of our brain was God given, because God wanted to communicate with us, and for us to share His Divine Plan.

The core statement of Kabbalah concerns its findings. There are 10 dimensions to all things and all is encompassed in the tree of Sefirot. At the level of numbers the Kabbalah and the string theory are in accord; the numbers of dimensions is ten. The essential teaching of Kabbalah is that God manifests through the Sefirot as the Tree of Life and the Tree of Light

The Beauty of Creation by Thought. The four noble truths

for God is the Divine light that reaches out to everyone and everything. There are ten branches holding the seven coloured chakra lights, starting with a red light at the bottom and working up through the colours of orange, yellow, green, blue, violet and white at the top where an angel sits.

When you achieve perfection, purity, harmony, love and absolute Truth, you will reach the top of the tree and pass into God's presence. A rainbow surrounds the tree and colours radiate onto the tree from all directions. The rays of the rainbow met together to produce another light, few have ever seen.

The Celestial Wishing Tree

Chapter Nine

Different Methods Used in Healing

There are numerous methods of healing. They are all based on :- love, comforting, reassurance, friendship, support, kindness, inner peace and happiness.

People that come for spiritual healing are people in pain, distress, terminally ill people. They have tried every form of medicine and it hasn't worked. If you have ever had terrible pain which goes on for months or years, you would know how desperate life becomes. Is it worth continuing with life? I have had people say to me, 'John, give me something to kill me.' Some people turn to religion for help. If you sincerely believe, this is a great idea, the right choice.

In India you will find healers using ancient customs and rituals, and yet they have found a way of healing. There is a saying that, 'the proof of the pudding is in the eating.' Do the spiritual centres perform miracles? Is sight restored, the deaf made to hear, the lame made to walk? No; reassurance is given, the rest is up to you. So some benefit is given, and to be healed the patient needs to believe healing will take place. The centres for healing do not instruct their healers to explain this to their patients, prior to healing. The patients are looking for someone to hear their troubles, someone who can share their grief, someone they can depend upon.

What distinguishes religion from other beliefs from moral codes, magic, ancient custom and rituals? Is it a belief that the absolute goodness overcomes the evil in the world? Is it a function of our brain in the balance of neurotransmitters sending messages along our brain cells?

Religion is an encyclopedia. We need to study all the religions to find a common denominator. The poor and needy may turn to religion for help. For a solitary man there may be a need to find comfort in a supreme being, and in bad health and dying the need to turn to someone for help. To quote schleiermachers, 'The essence of religion consists in the feeling of an absolute dependence.'

Spiritual healers will need to spend half an hour with your patients finding out medical histories, treatments and drugs used and other help your client has already received. What parts of the body need most attention, most energy? Which chakras control that area affected? Explain to your client that everything helps in healing or curing the cause. Explain everything in life comes under the Universal Law, cause and effect. You can spiritually heal the effect, but if you don't understand the cause the effect will come back. Introduce your client to other natural healings – a good diet, eat less, lose weight, stop smoking, drinking too much alcohol, consider taking vitamins, herbal remedies, homeopathy, acupuncture, Chinese medicines, Buddhist meditations.

The list is too long. You won't have time to cover it all. You can recommend books, for instance, some come from the doctor's surgery on diabetes, weight loss, cholesterol, heart attacks, symptoms of cancer. Males aged 50 and over may need reassurance on prostate cancer. But is all this too much? Is it too much for the healer to know? Healers like Betty Shine with extraordinary powers of connecting with the spirit world and help from spiritual doctors, spent much time understanding medical histories to perform healing from the spiritual sources. She has helped thousands of sick people.

I went to a display of spiritual healing at Newton Abbott where part of the grounds of the Race Course were cordoned off for the venue. Many tents displayed their crafts, selling everything from books, crystals, pictures of angels, lotus chairs, sound gongs and pipes, and healers everywhere all in competition with each other. For £3 you had 5 minutes healing, for £5, 10 minutes healing. It was like a supermarket, buy one, get one free. I expect they had to raise money to cover the cost of their stalls/stands and presentation of items for sale. They wanted to sell me a course of healing to attend. Most offers were introductory courses around

£85, 1st year course £185, 2nd year course £220. If you pass completion you will receive a certificate and you can pay to join their association and get legal protection in case you get sued. Can you imagine Jesus going to a firm of solicitors and saying I need protection in case I get sued?!

I went to one healer for 5 minutes.

She asked ‘Do you feel better?’

I replied that I didn’t feel bad in the first place.

She rebuffed me – ‘Don’t come back to me again. You’re not trying.’

I saw one healer, her client lying on a bed, the healer’s hands 3ft above the body making great arcs in the air and shouting in excitement. Was a demon coming out? I was told she was theatrical. Healers please refrain from such demonstrations.

All healers say they use the same force, the unseen energy that flows into and through all things in nature; this is the spiritual energy. They differ in the way they use it for healing. I met so many different ones I can only list a few and a brief description which may not be adequate, in which case I do apologise – Contact UK Healers, PO Box 207, Leeds, LS16 5WX telephone 0845 60 30 137 Email: admin@ukhealers.info Website: www.ukhealers.info for courses and healing.

1) REIKI

The Reiki master teacher learns how to give the patient this life energy, following a pattern he or she has been taught in a 3 year training, using symbols and mantras. This releases the energy to flow into the chakras. It is a hands-on procedure. Reiki may be continued with meditation.

2) QI GONG (Chinese) The South West branch hold a QI Gong camp on Dartmoor tel: 0845 456 1852 www.qigong-southwest.co.uk

It revitalizes the body, calms and focuses the mind, uplifts the spirit. Tied up with this thinking is the combined knowledge of Egyptian, Tibetan, Chinese Qi Gong, yoga and astrology. Mention is made of a ‘liquid lightbody’. It is based on ancient writings of Buddhists, Kabbalists, Taoists, for example and illuminates the journey from unconsciousness to enlightenment. I recommend reading Egyptian book of the Dead by Dr

Ramses Seleem ISBN 184181 109-2.

3) SHIATSU

Comes from Japan. Popular in the West since 1970. It can bring healing on an emotional, mental and spiritual level by manipulating the natural flow of energy along meridians for example. Shiatsu or finger pressure as the translation suggests uses different methods, the original Chinese massage was called ANMA massage, used in Japan 1000 years ago. In its assessment plan for treatment one hour is spent discussing medical history, life style, disharmony, diet, relaxing revitalizing treatment. Earlier in my text I said spiritual healers should spend half an hour with their clients doing all these things. They print a list of medical benefits reported by satisfied clients, for more information contact: Jean Netherway, 'Roots' Westerland, Marldon, Paignton, South Devon. Tel 01803 525447.

4) CRYSTAL HEALING

Can a healer with all electro magnetic radiation from our bodies interact with a crystal and how? Crystals do absorb certain energies and re-emit energies. If a given crystal can absorb positive energies from a healer and remit them to another this must be good in healing e.g. Copper bracelets help people with rheumatism. I recommend to read 'Crystal Power, Crystal Healing, The complete handbook' by Michael Gienger ISBN 071372677-6. It is well worth doing a course on crystal healing I recommend: Christine Morris, Crystal and Sounds Healing Teacher, 2 Stepps Cottage, Old Road, Harbertonford, Devon TQ9 7TE. Tel: 01803 732351 – mobile: 07813 754306

5) SOUND THERAPY

The association of Sound Therapy and Harmonic Studies – this association was founded in 1998 by Michele Averard and Nestor Kornblum, in order to establish standards in the practice of sound therapy in Spain. The primary aim is to spread the awareness and knowledge of sound as a powerful tool for personal and planetary transformation. Nestor and Michele, directors of the Association, conduct intensive courses on the therapeutic and transformative uses of sounds and particularly the voice, worldwide. Tel +3496 6482312 mobile +34686 942033 email:

info@harmonicsounds.com web site: http://www.harmonicsounds.com Soulnote – Gongs and singing bowls, Chinese and paste gongs, stands and mallets, singing bowls, tingshas, bells, playing wands, meditation CDs, workshops. Tel: 01626 895406. Email: info@soulnote.co.uk

6) The Natural Healing West Country Fellowship

WNHF Membership Secretary: Diana Edworthy. Tel: 01363 772550.

7) SHABDAN

PO Box 10070, Dundee, DD2 5YT. www.iona-light.co.uk Tel: 01382 581951

Shambhala and Shabdan are the next step in human consciousness. Under the guidance of Shambhala, Shabdan will present new techniques on a hand on heart lamps using Iona light, a revolution in consciousness.

8) The Enneagram Programme. Pattern of the Soul.

It shifts your vibration up to a higher level. It features on patternof the soul. Part 1 (2 days) gives detailed descriptions of the 9 personality types including what these real gifts are, what drives their behavior patterns, what holds them back etc. Courses in London and Devon. Tel: 01884 855759, www.enneagram-uk.com, enquiries@enneagram-uk.com

9) British Astrological and Psychic Society

They have a list of persons registered as consultants who practice (a) tarot (b) astrology (c) intuitive cards (d) runes (e) clairvoyance, mediumship, aura (f) palmistry (g) psychic art. Tel: 0906 4700827

10) Reflexology, Indian Head Massage, Aromatherapy

Bliss Holistics – 07730 560688 or 01803 782884. Info@theblissexperience.co.uk

11) Homeopathy

Has been practiced for 2000 years but was made more popular in 1810 by Samuel Hahnemann in a textbook ORGANON. It starts with a long interview discussing physical and emotional symptoms. Treatment is like with like in very dilute solution e.g. Scarlet fever produces fever, delirium, throbbing pains, hot dry red skin. Belladonna produces the same symptoms, so it is used. Leslie Gregerson, the principal of the London

School of Homeopathy tells me it's a long training, five years, and at the end students become members of the British Homeopathic Society. This doesn't stop people practicing it who are unqualified. Website: www.homeopathy –soh.com

Most spiritual healers advertise in one of the following magazines:-

1) Healing Today Tel 0845 1232777

2) Breathing Space magazine. 5 Market Street, Buckfastleigh, Devon, TQ11 0BA

3) National Federation of Spiritual Healers

4) The Energetic Quarterly www.share-international.org

5) Quest www.questuk.co.uk Tel: 01803 702674

6) The British Astrological and Psychic. Tel: 0906 4700827. PO Box 5687, Springfield, Milton Keynes MK6 3WZ

Some words teachers use may express a different meaning to them in the context of spiritual healing. Challenge what the teacher says. People are too ready to agree with a teacher because the teacher says so, and they want to get a certificate. Take the word 'transmutation. To a gifted medium with powers of clairvoyance this reflects the dictionary definition 'to change from one form to another'. To an average person in the street it is magic. It is a big step for the teacher to say it isn't magic without some explanations.

How would you react if teacher said, 'I want you to pair off and sit opposite each other. Now look behind the other person's eyes into their brain and make soul contact.'? The person you were opposite looks evil, full of hatred and bad tempered. No I don't wish to communicate with that soul. Our brains can be accessed by good and evil (bad) spirits. I don't want to open up my soul for some bad spirit to try and take over my mind and body.

Take the case of my friend, Verona, who was learning to do spiritual healing in San Rafael near San Fransisco. These are her own words. The experience that Verona Seiter had is an example of psychokenesis.

'I was learning to do energy work with an energy teacher. There are blocks of energy in a person and when you look at a person you learn to look at their energy pattern. You look for where the energy is blocked. You massage that particular part of the person's body.

'The first unusual thing that happened, my teacher was working on another person and I was standing watching her. She asked him if he felt any fear. He said 'no'. Then she asked him if he felt any anger. He denied that also. At that moment I started violently shaking from head to foot. My teacher looked at me and said 'let it go, it is not yours.' She told me that you have to let the other person's bad energy channel out through you and let it out, do not let it hang onto you.

'Then I started waking up on the night, sitting up and speaking in tongues; some tongues were old, some were young, speaking many languages through me. I could not stop it happening. It was no dream. This happened many times over a two week period. It scared me. During that same period I was massaging my daughter's neck. I did not think it counted as body work so I did not wash my hands up above my elbows in cold water. What happened next was scary. In the middles of the night I got blisters all over my body. These blisters did not hurt, then I went and washed my hands up to my elbow in cold water and said a prayer 'what have I done wrong?' I went back to sleep. When I woke up in the morning the blisters had gone, leaving some red marks.

'I went back to see my energy teacher and told her what had happened, and how scared I was. Speaking in tongues was still going on. She sent me to a medium. I had a session with her. She said some forces were trying to take over my body and I should go to a healer. In the medium's house I was causing doors and windows to rattle. The medium sent me back to my teacher who referred me to her teacher. I went to him still being sceptical about everything. He told me to close my eyes. You could feel his energy in his hands. He spoke softly and I felt a white light, very warming, go through me. This apparently took some time, but I was not conscious of it taking much time. Then he said 'sit up, it is finished'. It worked; I never had any more trouble, never spoke with any more tongues. I had been training for several months with about nine other people. I never went back and stopped doing energy work.'

Let's Examine Two Other Categories of Healing

1) Distance Healing and Colour Therapy and Healing

Matthew Manning is a good distance healer. His distance healing is studied by doctors who have examined his patients before and after healing. It works. The thought process carries the healing with positive energy and belief that it will happen. There are over 150 documented cases. His book *The Healing Journey* is well worth reading – ISBN 07499 22443 (hbk). Harry Edwards was another very famous distance healer. Betty Shine's achievements are recorded in her many books.

2) Colour Therapy and Healing

Vicky Wall's book *The Miracle of Colour Healing, Aura-Soma Therapy as the Mirror of the Soul* is a must. ISBN 085030895X. I believe so much talent comes from hard work, dedication and often suffering. I believe such talent has the backing of God, that some of us are preordained to serve. Divine wisdom is guiding and directing us.

Vicky had inherited gifts from her father and in her youth experienced spontaneous happenings, involving realization of auric sight and clairvoyance and healings. Her parents were deeply religious and practiced Kabbalah, the Torah; the innermost workings of God on earth. This Jewish belief extends from knowing God spoke to Moses on Mount Sinai 3400 years ago and believing this that God speaks to them in the same way. It covers the deep structure of the mind and it outer reality. I believe Vicky's father's revelations were displayed through the power of chakras and mystic practices.

Vicky said, 'My father has a knowledge of the medicinal and healing qualities of living plants and natural methods of healing which he passed on to me.'

I have always believed God gave us healing plants and fruits. Why are some fruits so brightly coloured? Because they want to attract you, they want to be picked. The skins of these fruits are high in anti-oxidants which are very good for you. The skins of black grapes grown at higher altitudes, are rich in anti-oxidants, like the Cabinet Sauvignon. Vicky said

I worked for a pharmacist and discovered the birth of aura-soma balance oils that were to heal and change the lives of so many and prove a mirror for the soul. Colour therapy embraces many live energies. It is a therapy that heals on all levels, physical, mental and spiritual that leads to other healings.

Automatic Writing and Spiritual Artwork

I have seen people with a spirit operating through them doing automatic writing. Some of it is very bizarre, nothing more than scratches on the paper, whilst some is more intelligent and may convey a message. The proof is in the quality of the message. There are many levels of spirits. Some are specialised. I knew Rosemary Brown (1916 – 2001). She was a spirit medium who claimed that dead composers dictated new musical works to her. Many musicians came to her and on many occasions Franz Liszt. I belong to the Liszt Society.

On one occasion when Louis Kentner, our president, was playing to us, Rosemary said to the man sitting between us, 'Liszt is here, he is sitting to the right of you.' My reply was 'Can you please ask Liszt to get off my knee?' She was investigated by neural experts, psychologists, paranormal investigators but the conclusion reached was music was being given to her.

The most famous case of automatic writing was the case of Pearl Curran and Patience Worth. A Louisiana housewife made contact with an entity named Patience Worth. The two collaborated for years and turned out entire novels and thousands of poems, all filled with material that the uneducated Curran could have known nothing about.

Betty Shine writes in her book *Mind to Mind*, 'There is no doubt in my mind that I have been taught by unseen people all my life. It is through this guidance that I have learned about mind energy, and that the mind and the personality survive the death of the physical body. I receive knowledge and healing from many different sources, and sometimes a voice speaks clearly to me. At other times information is impressed on my mind.'

Automatic writing is the process where writings appear without the conscious thoughts of the writer. Poems of great length and beauty arrive so quickly. This suggests someone is using the mind of a person doing the writing and this is the basis of psychokenesis. The Brazilian medium Chico Xavier wrote 400 books in the twentieth century. Divaldo Franco has written many books on peace, love, healing and education through spiritual writing, one book in a language with which he is not familiar. Jesus is one of he spiritual authors.

This is a message received through automatic writing;

'There is a *God* –Architect and Creator of the Universe. If one word were used to describe God, it would be *Love*.

'We human beings are in fact God's children; our soul (the true self, the seat of consciousness) having been created in God's image.

'As God's children, we were created with the potential to receive the actual essence of God's soul into our soul and to thus become transformed from the image of the divine into the very substance – at one with God, and conscious of our immortality.

'This 'divine essence' is God's personal love, which we call the *divine love.* It is separate and distinct from the 'natural love' that is manifest throughout God's creation, and comes into the soul only in response to sincere, heartfelt desire for its inflowing – in other words, in response to *prayer*. This love will not come into the soul without these prayers, for it is given only to those who *freely choose* to receive it.

'The transformation brought about by this love is gradual, the pace being determined by the frequency and 'soulfulness' of one's prayers for the love. There is a 'snow-ball effect' at work also – each inflowing of the love bringing with it an increase in *faith*, making it progressively easier to aspire for the love.....'

Meditation

Meditation is how to relax the mind and achieve a state of inner contentment and peace, which is so calming and beneficial to the health of everyone. What a lovely state to achieve as a spiritual healer before you start work with a client, because you can pass on this inner peace. It is mind control and can bring about relief from anxieties and in many ways heal ourselves from depressive and life-threatening illnesses. The Buddha reached enlightenment through meditation. You must clear your mind of negative thoughts and relaxing in your lotus chair, close your eyes, breathe deeply and evenly and enter a dream like state. Brain activity shuts down and this allows your mind to wander to things of beauty.

Start with imagining a field of beautiful flowers. What can you see? The colours are beautiful because the divine white light that has entered them is broken down into the seven colours of the rainbow. The seed is perfect and so is the flower in shape, colour and fragrance. This aroma is mixing with the aroma of the other flowers nearby, as if the flowers are talking to each other and to the grass and trees. This is the aura-soma therapy giving colour healing. Insects visit the flowers and nature is secure in the never ending desire to pollinate, reproduce and create. Finally the flowers produce fruits for us to eat.

Learn to relax the body. How to do this is in the book *A Guide to Meditation* by Lorraine Turner ISBN 0-75257-198-2.

Musical sounds are relaxing and sound therapy can heal. Imagine you are relaxing in the garden, lying on a mattress on green grass, your head on a pillow, surrounded by the colours of many flowers. Imagine you can hear the sounds of a distant choir singing Puccini melodies drifting across the field. This is truly relaxing. You are creating mantras, affirmations to be repeated with the sound of music which resonates through your body to bring about a transformation of consciousness. Mantras help to achieve a state of peace and tranquility, to focus your mind and thereby increase awareness, alertness and creativity. Buddhists, Muslims and Christians have used mantras for thousands of years, chanting GOD, in Hindu AUM, chanting love, chanting alleluia. Create your own mantras.

You can combine regular breathing with mantras and explore the meanings of the chakras and their colours. Visualisation uses imagination to create well-being. Allow your visualisation to incorporate all five senses. Use a lighted candle to develop your concentration. Put on your favourite CD and listen to relaxing music. The contentment of your mind is now ready to pass on to others in your healing work.

Faith Healing

Do you remember reading about creation from lectures Baird Spalding's team of scientists had in the middle room of the Taw Cross Temple? Translation from the copies of the ancient Babylonian tablets recorded, 'From the darkness came the great white and gold light, with intelligence and form to create.' This intelligence appointed God to create and run planet Earth in the ideal way the Divine Principle held in mind, and gave him all the attributes of the Divine Principle. God moved on the Divine white light to create. That is the same beam of white light that entered my brain flashing with great brilliance when I went to a spiritual healer on the Isle of Wight. That is the same white light that can be photographed by Kirlian photography.

When Divaldo Franco was doing divine spiritual healing on epileptic patients under a team of neurological researchers who were filming, they saw a small white light at the top of the brain, at the crown chakra. That is the divine spiritual energy. This white light imparts to the 7 chakras and the 7 colours of the rainbow. The same white divine light enters flowers and all living things and gives flowers their colours, design and beauty.

Jesus said love is very important in healing and belief and faith that you will be healed.

In the Bible a man said to Jesus, 'Lord I am not worthy to receive you but only say the word and I shall be healed.'

Jesus said to many people 'Great is your faith and your faith has made you whole.'

People wanted to touch his garments to be cured of their illness.

In Tibet there is a healing temple about 800 miles from Calcutta. Pilgrims go there to be healed. Baird Spalding and his team of eleven scientists went there in 1895 to investigate. There were no attendants, no monks, no priests, everyone walked through or were carried through the temple. The healing vibrational energies were so high everyone going in the temple, believing, was healed, healed permanently. No bad words could be said in the temple. The voice box didn't work. Ever since the temple had been built 800 years ago the vibrational energy level was maintained so high anyone going in can be healed. If we would create this energy level around us, could we heal ourselves? Yes I am certain we could. This is how it was when man had syntax first and the ability to talk to God and access His divine spirit in the cells in our brain that receive the divine mind.

Some of Jesus' Miracles of Healing

Mark 1:23-27	Evil spirit commanded to leave a man
Mark 1:40-42	Jesus healed a man with leprosy
Mark 2 :3-5	Jesus cures a paralytic
Luke 8:1-3	Several women cured of evil spirits and diseases, one of them was Mary Magdalene from whom seven spirits had come out
John 9:1-41	Blind man from birth. Jesus spat and made mud and rubbed into his eyes. Go and wash in the pool of Siloam and the man saw.

Other Miracles not confined to healing the sick

1. Walking on the water
2. Feeding the 5000 – Luke 9:12-17
3. Calming the seas in a boat – Mark 4:35-41
4. Turning the water into wine
5. Accelerating nature – the harvest ripened early.

Many miracles happened spontaneously. Jesus raised Lazarus from the dead. Lazarus didn't say I am dead but I believe you can bring me back to life.

Evangelical means Christian belief associated with the importance of a personal relationship with Jesus and commitment to a life shaped by the Bible. Evangelism means being enthusiastic to tell other people about the bible and find faith in Jesus. The Salvation Army is an example of an evangelistic movement. Their determination and courage is outstanding, reflecting the dynamic thinking of its founder William Booth.

If you do any form of spiritual healing work you must know some of the Universal Laws. If you have had a calling and you wish to go abroad to do missionary work, going abroad will introduce you to different cultures and different services of worship. The Anglican churches are scattered throughout the world in 45 provinces. I have included a map of the world showing Christian worship which accounts for 33% of the World's population or 2.1 billion people.

Muslims are next in number 21% of the world's population or 1.3 billion people. Hinduism accounts for 1 billion, Buddhists and Chinese Traditionalists 400 million, and several others in lesser numbers. Judaism is the religion of the Jewish people and they support the Old Testament of the Bible. There are Jewish Christians living in Jerusalem that support the New Testament. Jews traditionally believe in the first five books of the Old Testament, Genesis, Exodus, Leviticus, Numbers and Deuteronomy, and that they were written by Moses after God talked to Moses in the Sinai Deseret. Some Jews stay with their roots, the Kabbalah and the Torah - the words spoken by God to Moses. They believe God will talk to them if they achieve perfection. Some have been endowed with gifts of healing.

Some of the Bible suffers from mistranslation. The original Hebrew chronology is intact. The ten tribe house of Israel was divided into two, the House or Kingdom of Israel and the tribe of Judah. Not all the tribe of Judah were from Israel and Abraham, Isaacs and Jacob were not Jews. The ten tribe House of Israel were not referred to as Jews. The Jews were a tribe of the Israelite nation. Those that are known to us today as Jews are the remnants of the tribe of Judah that returned to Palestine after they were released from captivity. Jews today are less than 1 third blood of the real tribe of Judah. Where the Jews have lived and mingled with the

Israelites or Aryan they have flourished. You can trace the migration of Israel from Jerusalem, some settling in the British Isles. The tribe of Dan are identified by the Danube River. Other tribes are Danes, Jutes, Picts and Jews are all over the globe.

In 1300 BC Abraham was commanded by God to lead his Jewish people from UR in Mesopotamia to Canaan and Egypt, the Great Exodus. There is a large and well illustrated book, 'Mapping the History of World Religions' by Dr Ian Barnes ISBN 978 184 573 356-8. In his book Judaism and Christianity are extensively studied with maps of the journeys of St Paul and the early spread of the Gospel.

The Japanese and Chinese come from the Motherland of Mu, and were called Uiguar, or wandering tribes. They formed a high level of civilization in cities in the Gobi Desert 200,000 years ago. They worshipped the true principle and lived close to the spiritual body, accessing their needs from universal substance and universal energy. They recorded their truths in 12 bibles cut into stones in their motherland.

Jesus' mother was Mary and his father Joseph, representing descendants of David, the true light bearer from the seed of Abraham, meaning Ah Brahm, the bearer of the complete light from the great cosmos.

Going abroad, will your evangelical missionary work be received well by the community you wish to visit? They may resist change. The church you decide to go to may be unkept, broken windows, leaking roof, unfriendly welcome. You cannot hear the worship above the noise of badly behaved children and a church with no flowers. They may have their own prayer book different to the one used by the Anglican Church in England. There is a great diversity in church services. There are great disagreements in church matters. Jesus condemns inter denominational bickering. Some Gospel churches are very evangelical in their services and wave their hands in the air making lots of noises and clapping their hands. Most of the churches have a visitor's pamphlet so you can follow the service. In some Christian churches there is no Cross of Jesus, no altar, no celebrations at Christmas or Easter. They may not have the sacrament, but still have the Bible readings and lively discussion groups discussing the Bible. The feeling of the community spirit is high.

Christianity has 33% of the World's population but there is much diversity within religion. When I go into a church I look for how many have attended and what welcome I get. Later I consider the standard of the service and the message from the sermon.

Sometimes religions opposed the forward movement of science. Take the case of the Roman Catholic Church opposing the views of Galileo (1564 – 1642). Galileo observed the solar system and made telescopes and microscopes. The Church held the view the Earth was the centre of the universe, which God had made especially for us. In 1995 they apologized for keeping Galileo under house arrest for 20 years. In the Reformation of the Church in 1546 period they burn the 3 great libraries of books in Alexandra containing a history of the World. The World population is 6 billion. We are running out of food and energy. We need to reduce the World population. Birth control must be exercised. If a Church has been stupid in the past, how can we trust it in the future?

The Roman Catholic Church operates a good family church and reliable church services with the Sacraments. They care for their congregation and support education for their young children.

The Church of England and Roman Catholic Churches have similar services. Catholicism believes in many manifestations in contact with mankind, reincarnations, visions, apparitions, guardian angels, emancipation of the soul during life. Demons are called evil spirits. The Church of England and Rome have Bishops who officiate at services to cast out devils, service of exorcism.

Christians, Jews and Muslims have all worshipped in Jerusalem. They all have elaborate places of worship. Let's hope they always will have, and present disputes can be resolved. Muslims distrust the West; hardly surprising when American and the British have killed a million people in Iraq and Afghanistan. There is no place for terrorism in the World. Terrorists disturb World peace. Iran supplies arms to the Iraqis to keep the war going. It is only a very small number of Muslims who encourage terrorism. They are religious people, praying 5 times a day. No way do they collectively want a major war. They all want to go to Mecca at least once in a life time. They don't want to see their mosques bombed. They say God talks to them especially at their most holy site, Mecca. The message given to them 1400 years ago was, 'the way to enlightenment is knowledge, intelligence and creativity.' They have brought more inventions and progress to the lands that they have inhabited than any of their neighbours have achieved.

There is now diversity in their religion centering on the interpretations of the Qur'an. The heads of their religion say there can be no changes. Others say we must adapt to changing societies. In 1972 women never wore headgear in Cairo. Now all women wear headgear and some cover their faces completely. What if they don't want to wear headgear? They are not allowed to appeal, they are not allowed to express their point of view, because men write the rules, and failure to observe them could lead to flogging. Women are not allowed in many mosques. It's for men only. Iran has a record of terrible punishments for disobeying the rules. They have a different concept of Human Rights. A woman who has a baby outside of wedlock is stoned to death. Common punishments include cutting off hands and feet, floggings, hanging by the neck, decapitation. It keeps the population in order. Their threats to kill Christians are alarming. Strapping bombs to themselves to blow up communities, to cause chaos, terrible suffering, terrible grief; a primitive reversal to animal thinking and behavior. Religion is about love not hatred.

The Messages from the Baird Spalding Voyages with the Grand Masters over a three year period. **The spiritual messages were predestined to happen. The storyline helped to convey the messages. This is true throughout Baird Spalding's Volumes 1, 2 and 3.**

It was predestined to happen from the first time Baird met Emil in the park at Calcutta to the return to Darjeeling 3 years later. Many of the names in the happenings are people who are Grand Masters, people that have taken their bodies with them, live on the celestial realm with Jesus, and can come and go in their earthly physical bodies, and using the powers of their spiritual body. The most important people illustrated in the story were Jesus, Emil, Emil's mother who lived close to Jesus in the celestial realm, Jast, Nephrow and many others including Buddha and high priests, and grand Lamas.

What was told to us began and finished with a life well lived, a life lived close to the spiritual world and the achievements. From the lessons came the truth and deep meaning behind the truth. Everyday tasks are much easier if we follow the examples they gave us. It requires a knowledge of achievements in spirit and an understanding that universal laws can never be changed. It tells us everything came from energy, the divine white light and made into material form, a low density form of matter.

The whole story is like a re-enactment of the New Testament. Emil was known to Baird Spalding's family generations before. Emil is at least 650 years old. Many pages of writings were instructions from Jesus, Emil and Emil's mother and others. The message behind everything is that there is no death, the spiritual body lives on, creation is continuous, intelligence, achievements and perfection must be worked for. There are alternative ways of accessing every need from the Universal Substance and asking correctly, knowing your request will be answered. The miraculous happenings all pointed to finding maps and details of the lost cities in the Gobi Desert.

These maps and locations were found in many places in India and Tibet. The expedition arrived in the Gobi Desert at the end of June 1895. Mine shafts were sunk. The first one opened a chamber at 45 feet and a vault at 95 feet. This revealed much treasure, gold, statues and indications of a people living in great knowledge close to spiritual life. The human brain had enlarged three times its size in two million years. This gave us syntax, the ability to put words into sentences for recalling and our subsequent enormous computing powers. God made man intelligent and this is the different between man and animals. God wanted to share his knowledge with his Divine Children. This must have happened about 300,000 years ago.

Some of their messages of spiritual religious significance

Your body has an invisible life fluid, the product of interactions between the spiritual and physical bodies. If you lead a debauched life of alcohol, drugs, stealing, killing, you dissipate the life fluid and degenerate to animal levels. If you lead a good honest life you preserve the life fluids. If the life force in conserved, the body cells change for new ones as readily at 500 years old as at 10 years old. Your life fluid is many times more vital than a corresponding amount of pure blood. About you is an abundance of Universal Substance which you can draw on e.g. Jesus feeds the 5000. You have specialist cells in your brain that receive impulses from the Divine Mind. By raising your vibrational energy rate and by pleasing God and Jesus with true thought from the heart, you can communicate with Jesus and the Grand Masters in the celestial realm. Jesus abides only to be of service as do all great souls. The true mystery of life is to express God through the Christ in the individual.

The spirit of God shines forth from the heart. I can enter the Kingdom of God and that Kingdom is right within us. Be pure in thought, strive for perfection and substitute hate for love. If you forgive men that trespass against you, your heavenly Father will also forgive you.

Jesus erased the false image in the consciousness of the one to whom he ministered. He raised the vibrations of his body by connecting his thoughts with the Divine Mind. By seeing the divine perfection for all he raised the vibrations of the one he healed until the image of imperfection was entirely erased.

In the first year the team of eleven scientists were in Calcutta studying the routes and planning the journey to the Gobi Desert. Emil met Baird in the park and offered to help. He displayed extraordinary abilities, from talking to birds, animals, appearing behind locked doors, solving Bairds' journey problems one by one. The team moved to Northern India and prepared to leave from a village called Potal for short voyages in the first year. Emil arrived and gave instructions for their final journey of 90 miles to Asmah which would take 5 days. Two fine Hindu men organised and came with this first voyage, Jast and Neprow. Emil transported his body to Asmah in no time and was there to meet them when they arrived.

Emil appeared that evening in the midst of them without opening the door. He explained, 'I held my body in the universal by raising its vibrations and it returned to the universal, where all substance exists. Through my Christ consciousness 'I AM', I held my body in my mind until its vibrations were lowered and it took form in this room. Jesus enters the room as I have done.'

The next journey, only 20 miles was to a small village. Jast accompanied them. As they entered the village all the villagers came out to meet them. Jast took them to a clearing surrounding the village. He appeared uneasy. A short distance into the jungle they came upon the form of a man lying on the ground as though dead. As Jast walked toward it, the figure became animated and rose to a standing position. It was Jast and instantly two joined together as one. He laid his body down to protect the village and its inhabitants from marauding men and animals. From that moment onwards they all lost all fear of death.

Emil continues, 'There is no reason why your body should not grow as young and vital as the vital seed from which it sprang. There is no natural law of death for man. Joyous thoughts, love thoughts, and ideal thoughts create the beauty called youth. Learn to smile. A smile from the soul is spiritual relaxation. Jesus saw the heavens were opened unto Him, and he saw the wonderful law of expression whereby ideas conceived the Divine Mind come forth into expression and manifest as form.'

They journeyed northwards to the Healing Temple. I estimate this to be 350 miles from where they left Potal in North India. Baird Spalding said it was 800 miles from Calcutta to the temple. Since no maps are included in his books it is difficult to locate places mentioned in the text. They encountered a terrible storm on this voyage and had to take shelter for several days. They ran short of food. Emil produced 40 loaves from the Universal Substance.

The Healing Temple is open to the public at all times. Only words of love and peace have ever been spoken, and the thought of harmony and perfection. No bad words can be spoken in the temple. The vibrational energy level is too high. The fabric of the building has absorbed so much love and healing energy that anyone passing through it is healed by its radiation. Curious people who do not believe will not receive any help. They observed and 90% of those healed were healed permanently.

It was the end of June 1894. July 4th was fast approaching, a day to remember for Americans. Thoughts came of completed works done in the past, and the excitement of a new age dawning, the age of crystal, the pure white light of God. E Pluribus unum = unity out of diversity = university. Every good desire man has is God's desire. Divine man is deathless, external. The Grand Masters were constantly instructing them. Emil's mother told them, the next exciting event in man's understanding is coming soon. His conscious vibrational energy rate from the top of his head will be raised, and this will allow him to see and talk to the next dimension. I have watched Divaldo Franco do this. He can see and talk to the next life.

Next day Baird Spalding, Emil and Jast went on a two day trek to an ancient temple, 12,000 years old, one of the first temples erected by the Siddha teachers. On the way back they were caught in a fire and surrounded by flames. Emil raised the vibrations of their bodies above those of a fire. A hole opened up in the flames and they walked through without any harmful effects.

Baird said to Emil, 'Your clothes are never dirty.'

He replied, 'This may seem remarkable to you but it seems more remarkable to us that one speck of God's created substance adheres to another of God's creations where it is not wanted and where it does not belong.'

Emil invited all to his home near Chungga Village, and to meet his relatives. They journeyed to Emil's home in a narrow gorge with a waterfall. All of Emil's relations had gathered. Emil explained that the heating and lighting in the room was provided by a universal force, we might understand as perpetual motion. This God Power is available for all to use. It will drive all mechanical devices and complete transportation, without using any fuel.

They received instructions. Their hostess resumed, 'We are able to throw thought vibration into the atmosphere which connect with the thought vibrations of those that have passed, and our vibrations collect those of the thoughts gone before until they draw them together at a given point. Then you are able to see those scenes reproduced just as they were when the scenes occurred. These scenes we are showing you are not produced photographically and mechanically.'

They were taken on a tour of the Taw Cross Temple and shown ancient tablets, copies of Old Babylon tablets, which they were taught to translate. This occupied them for many months. There were descriptions of the lost cities in the Gobi Desert. They were now discovering many references from different sources telling them of their ancient lost cities. Many miraculous happening occurred in the Taw Cross Temple. While they were receiving instruction, Jesus came into the room and shook hands with all of them. They photographed Him. He was surrounded by a white light, which cast no shadows. The Taw Cross Temple was used to store these copies of ancient Babylonian tablets. The tablets measured 24 inches by 14 inches and 2 inches thick. There was an elderly man who translated the tablets. He was called the man of the records.

They received further instructions. No man can confer any rights upon another. Prayer that is always answered must be true prayer, therefore must be scientific and if scientific operates according to fixed laws.

In the Taw Cross Temple the old man of the records died. Jesus and Emil appeared. Jesus said he was so close to achieving his mission that we should give him the chance to complete his life's work. Jesus came and put his soul back into him. The man from the records disappeared from view. Two of their party had been holding hands. He returned with every vestige age gone.

He began to speak. 'Dear ones you cannot know the joy, the peace, the great bliss you have given me in awakening me as you have. Just a moment ago it was all dark; I stood, fearing to go on and yet I could not return. The only way I can explain it is I seemed engulfed in a great blackness from which I suddenly seemed to awake and now I am again with you.'

His face became so radiant with joy that there was no mistaking his sincerity.

The messages from these teachings are many. God puts the soul into the new born baby at birth to give it life. You can never lose the level of soul attainment. You can ask to be reborn (reincarnation) to complete your soul's rise to the highest aspirations of Truth and Accomplishment. Jesus said, 'The Christ was when God created the first man in His own image and likeness.'

Emil says, 'The greatest cure for in harmony is the knowledge that it is not from God, that God never did create it.'

The thought process and its accomplishment are very important, but if the thought is immediately withdrawn so those particular vibrations are not fixed, they cannot be projected. We are able to receive and send out the same True and Divine vibrations that we receive from the Divine Mind. We do not have the Divine Mind, but we have the cells that receive and project the vibrations of the Dive Mind.

If you separate yourself from God in thought, you will also separate yourself from him in manifestation. You will find that by fixing your thoughts and attention steadfastly on God and His Divine Perfection, you can raise the vibrations of your body so that they will blend harmoniously with those of the Divine Perfection that you are absolutely one with the Divine Perfection and thus one with God. God has nothing to do with sin, sickness, inharmony of man. Man himself brought them into being and man is the only one who can erase or forgive them. Sickness is not punishment sent from God. The emphasis is on man to cure his own sickness.

The voyage to the Gobi desert was an enormous undertaking, and could not have happened without the help from the Grand Masters. About 800 miles had to be covered to get to the Gobi Desert and then the return trip to Chungga Village. They left in the third week of April 1895 and returned by December 1895 covering 1600 miles. There are no maps of routes taken. The distance of 800 miles was covered from 23 April to 30 June. There were six days of stoppages with encounters with armed robbers and bad storms, and a further one week rest period toward the end of their journey. If they averaged 18 miles per day they could have arrived by 20th June.

The most likely route would be down the Giama Nu Chu Valley and then turn east toward Shigaste, and taking the Friendship Highway by the north route which runs about 50 miles west of Lhasa. With trading routes to China these routes would have been well established. They travelled in horse drawn caravans, on horseback, and on foot, with yaks carrying tents, food and water, and equipment. They arrived at the ancient city of the Uiqurs on 30 June and set to work in excavating.

At 90ft they broke into a large room and found gold, silver, bronze and clay statues, all beautifully wrought. They moved onto the next site and found at 45ft evidence of former civilisation. They moved to a third site which they had map references in detail and found more remains and rich in treasure. It is very evident that the history of these people is the history of the Aryan race, and we have been able to date these cities at 230,000 years BC. How long Baird Spalding then took to find the lost cities and finish their excavation is not recorded, but I expect they spent July and August on the work. Then they set off on their return journey in September, stopping at different villages for a period of time. Emil had invited them to spend winter at Chungga Village and they arrived in December. This would give them time to finish the translation of the tablets in the Taw Cross Temple before setting off in the spring to journey to Lhasa and have an audience with His Holiness the Dalai Lama.

It is recorded that ancient temples were used to store history and documents, like libraries today. Ancient writings would have been recorded on clay tablets and stone. The peoples of the lost cities in the Gobi worshipped in the open and lived very spiritual lives in touch with God. They lived to a great age.

The following year after Easter, the party prepared for their journey to Lhasa to visit the Potala Palace, the home of His Holiness the Dalai Lama. They travelled down the Giama Nu Chu Valley to the Tonjnor Jung Pass and followed the Tsan Pu River to Lhasa. The deeper spiritual head of Lhasa is the Buddha. As we approached the monastery the High Priest came out to meet us and to our surprise Emil and his mother were with him. We were received by the Dalai Lama. All this is recorded in volume 3 from pages 78 – 108. The beauty of the decorated marble tablets is described and also the incredible journey of 40 years from the time of their discovery in a Persian temple remains by a wandering priest to the time of their arrival at Potala Palace.

An old Lama casually remarked, 'Two of your associates who left you last summer will arrive in Calcutta at 1.30pm today, and if you wish to communicate with them, you can do so.' Baird Spalding wrote a message instructing them to go directly to Darjeeling and await their arrival on 24th August. They did meet them on 24th August in Darjeeling.

They left Lhasa to continue their journey to the Pora-Tat-Sang Monastery. They stayed at Xigaze, at the second largest Buddhist monastery in Tibet, the Tashilhumpo Monastery. This Lama is the next in charge after the Dalai Lama. There were 3000 monks in residence. When they left Baird Spalding told them they were joined by a laughing Chela, who made their journey much easier. They journeyed through the Phari Pass and saw Everest. On the other side of the pass was a beautiful valley called Chubi and they followed a trail by way if Tachi-Chu-Jong entering a forest with songbirds and wild fowl. They stopped at Maha Muni a fortress like temple at 16,000 feet. Eventually they arrived at Pra-ta where there was a large gathering of peoples, numerous temples, large caves, Yogis, Sadhus, Gurus and many others Yogi Santi passed them hot food, made an address and found them accommodation. The next day they went to Pora-tat-sanga monastery and met the Master Puriji. Beliefs are not shared by Lamas and Yogis. The Yogis cannot believe the teaching of any one man can be final. He sees that every human being has access to all knowledge right within himself.

They went up to the temple of the Pora-tat-sanga by rope and bucket type transportation. In the morning Master Puriji had placed a stairway for them to walk down from a height of 75 feet. When they came to go back up there was no stairway. They went back up by standing on a flat rock and this was raised by levitation, no ropes, no visible signs of how it happened. Master Puriji taught them how to say AUM (God) and when everyone chanted AUM the rocks vibrated with the energy. They went from cave to cave and talked to many of the Yogis and Sadhus, who had lived in caves for years, being looked after by Universal Substance and energy, living in spiritual enlightenment. When they left they demonstrated great powers of healing.

Pora-tat-sanga

The sound of the Universe has continued from there for eons along with some other interesting phenomena which Western minds cannot accept, even speaking with people oversees and locally, that had actually been to the temple Pora-tat-sang. The temple burnt down back in March of 1998. It is now called Tak Sang. Tak Sang Monastery or goes by the name Tigers Lair.

Lamas belief is in Buddha to reach Buddha enlightenment. Wandering Lamas go trekking without money or food. They converse with each other over long distances by soul contact called ATMA. On the morning they left there was an address by Master Puriji who declared, 'There is only one God,' and thousands of voices seem to join in with a chorus praising God. They spent two weeks at Pora-tat and were sad to leave. They travelled 70 miles to Sansrawar and rested at a temple near a lake for two days. Song birds sang from trees all about them. They went on the Muktinath with Yogi Santi and the laughing Chela, and were met by Emil and a number of his friends. They journeyed on to Hardwar. After a month of other stops and miraculous happenings they all met up at Darjeeling on 24th August 1896. They had been travelling four months from the Giama Nu Chu Valley to Lhasa, to Gynatze, to Pora-tat to Hardwar and Darjeeling. Here they studied each other's writings of events to record the message five that they had learnt.

Pora-tat-sanga

Tatoo Manu Asi? Suham = Do you have God inside you? Suham = God is inside me

The teacher says to the student 'Thou are God' and the student replies 'That I am, Su-ham.' Two consonants S and H are silent leaving AUM.

Master Puriji Explains: 'The right use in Hindustani is A-U-M, where A is a guttural sound, which starts in throat. To pronounce U the lips must be thrust forward. M is formed by pressing the lips together causing a resonant tone like the humming of a bee. A, the first part of AUM, contemplates GOD in the wakeful sense. U, the second part of AUM, obtains glimpses of the inner world and is of Spirit. M, the third part of AUM, sees God as Himself, becomes illuminated and is free immediately. Meditation upon AUM, the highest self is for everyone to say'

Pora-tat-sanga

Recovery work continues at ancient temple burnt down back in March of 1998. It is now called Tak Sang, or goes by the name of Tigers Lair.

The Tigers Lair, built high on a granite cliff outside the central Bhutanese town of Paro, is the most sacred temple in a country where Buddhism remains a powerful force in daily life.

It is reputed to have been built over a cave where a famous eighth-century Buddhist monk from Tibet, Guru Rimpoche, spent months in meditation. Buddhist legend says he rode to the spot on the back of a tiger to do battle with evil spirits.

An official who visited the site said many treasures may be recoverable, including priceless Buddhist texts, icons and elaborate silk paintings, which were feared lost.

The restoration of the Taktshang Monastery was commanded by His Majesty the King soon after the fire disaster in 1988 AD. It was a royal command that the original aura, authenticity and architectural splendor must be preserved at all cost. The project was immediately mobilized to restore the monastery and to preserve and strengthen Bhutan's unique spiritual heritage.

Guru Pema Jungney statue installed Taktshang

A gilded statue of Guru Pema Jungney became the first nangten (religious treasure) to be installed in the recently completed Guru Tshengyed Lhakhang of the Taktsang monastery.

The statue, three foot tall and weighing about 100 kilograms, was offered to Taktshang monastery by Her Majesty the Queen Mother, Ashi Kesang Wangmo Wangchuck.

The statue was installed and consecrated on February 27, 2002 coinciding with the auspicious 15th day of the Second month of the Bhutanese calendar.

So far the outer structure of six lhakhangs – Dubkhang, Guru Sungjoen Lhakhang, Guru Tshengyed Lhakhang, Dorji Drolo Lhakhang, Tsepamed Lhakhang and Nebi lhakhang (dedicated to the local deity Taktshang Singye Samdrup) – had been completed and three sertogs (gilded tops) had been installed.

Taktshang Monastery

Guru Pema Jungney statue

Meanwhile the fabrication work of the seventh lhakhang, the Chortern Lhakhang, is completed. The Kuenrey (common hall), a common kitchen and toilets will also be constructed. About 140 people, excluding skilled craftsmen picked from 18 dzongkhags, were engaged in the reconstruction of the monastery which was destroyed by fire in 1998. The reconstruction of Taktshang monastery began in April, 2000. It is now finished. I took these two photographs climbing to the Monastery in 2007.

Chapter Ten

The Spiritual World, Survival of the Soul, Death and Reincarnation, Conclusions

Man can work with nature in a higher rate of vibration than that in which nature works in the lower order of concept.

'Lift up your eyes and look on the fields, for they are white ready to harvest.' St John 4.35.

All is vibration and corresponds to the plane or field upon which vibration acts. If we attune our body consciously to a higher vibratory rate, we become those vibrations. Why does the word God have so much power? It is because of the vibrations that are released when the word is spoken, as it is the very highest vibration, God. Birds can sing at 25,000 vibrations a second and much more.

It is necessary to expand your consciousness to be the God Consciousness. This is part of the new race consciousness that is evolving to take in greater expanses of universal thought. God wants to manifest through you. You must be aware of your Divine nature as you are by inheritance a Christ of God.

The spiritual world is at a much higher vibrational frequency level. Access to the physical world from the spiritual world is difficult because the physical world is too dense. Access can occur in sound vibration. Verona, my girlfriend who died 4th August 2005 after a long illness, was a Shakespearean actress in San Fransisco and a trained singer from London School of Music. She has kept in touch with me on two occasions by singing to me.

Do like spirits attract? I believe so. The spirits of children can play with the spirits of other children, and at this level the spirits of children living on planet Earth can play with spirits in the next life. This has been well documented by Divaldo Franco. The next life is full of spirits in many forms. There are spirits that have attained the highest level of perfection, others on course to achieving perfection with determination, and lowly spirit forms which appear to enjoy wrong doing and are not intelligent.

Where do all these spirits come from? There are billions of inhabited planets in God's Universe all at different stages of creation. They come from there. We are all one big happy family under God's presence and direction. Read Allan Kardec's *The Spirits Book*, ISBN 978 8598161-18-7.

Many mediums have contributed knowledge from the spirit world. There are consistencies in representation of how things are and messages received. This is the classification given spirits into three principle groups:-

3rd Order – Imperfect Spirits

They are ignorant, evil, selfish and do not comprehend God. There is another subdivision of these spirits into a further five categories.

2nd Order – Good Spirits

The desire to be good, but still not totally removed from their material desires or corporal existence. They do denounce evil words of hatred, envy, jealousy etc. Also known as guardian spirits, beneficent deities. Again they are divided into four types.

Final Order – Pure Spirits

They are not subject to reincarnation, live eternally in the heart of God. Teach other spirits, help others in distress, also called angels, archangels and seraphim.

Spirits have a very fine covering called the perispirit. Perhaps the colour of the perispirit is related to their level of attainment, reddish hue starting with a lower order, moving up the chakra colours to purple and at the very top, white. The white light appears around Jesus. Angels are spirits of colour and beauty. Every living thing has a spirit.

Question – do spirits exert any influence over the events of life?

Answer – certainly because they counsel you. They add to your thought only in accordance with Divine Law.

Question – do we have a guardian angel that looks after us?

Answer – yes it is so.

I only hope any spirits around me are good spirits. Take the case of Verona Seiter doing healing work when evil spirits accessed her brain and tried to take her over. Very good spirits which have reached the highest perfection receive orders from God to teach throughout the Universe and supervise their execution. It is an extraordinary concept but it follows that if we send teachers to other parts of the universe, they can come here.

Was Quetzalcoati in 900 AD such a teacher from another planet reincarnated on Earth? It is said he knew everything and was worshipped as a God, and he said he would come back to Earth again.

The nature of the soul is considered by Aristotle. 'The brain has two functions:-the function of operating the body organs, eating to fuel the furnace within us by which heat and nourishment reach our body organs, and waste products are disposed of, and the higher centre of the brain the psyche which consists of two parts: - part one is the development of characteristics acquired by habits (Greek Ethos); part two is the strive toward complete happiness, which varies from man to man but emphasizes that the ergon (activity) demands of a man that he strive to make great achievements. This forms his total psyche which passes with him into the next life. This is enhanced by wisdom to understand intellectual excellence and a good moral code. In achieving these higher states the partition between the next life and this comes closer. It is that the God who made is, may have made us in a similar image and wants us to develop to higher levels. Communication to God through the psyche has altered our brains to this larger size.'

Psyche in Greek can mean butterfly. It resembles the struggle on planet earth for man entombed in his material body and then learns to rise into this beautiful meaning of the spiritual body.

What does the Bible say? God made man in his own image. Jesus said, 'When you have seen me you have seen my Father.' In the Old Testament God spoke to Jeremiah, 'Before I formed you in the womb I knew you, before you were born I set you apart. I appointed you as a prophet to the nations.' God selected Jeremiah's soul to be reborn which is known as reincarnation. Is our life mapped out for us from the time of birth?

Certainly it is if we are a chosen one of God. Do our grandparents, our relatives from times before us, plan for us on our return? Some religions and beliefs think so such as Hindus. Are all souls looking for a physical body for rebirth? When God selected Jeremiah's soul from rebirth was the soul at a high level of attainment? Yes I believe so. The highest level of attainment which we have achieved is in levels listed in His creation downwards from the Divine principle.

The spirit and the soul are the same. The soul lives in us and leaves on death to continue in the next life. The mind feeds the soul with life through our actions, so vividly displayed in Betty Shine's book *Mind Magic*. The God mind is the Divine Mind. We have specialist cells in our brain to receive instructions from the Divine Mind.

We are all divine because we are descended from the perfect child God made, the Christ child. Jesus called the Holy Spirit down from heaven to be in his disciples so they could heal the sick, do the miracles he did, and preach the word of God throughout the lands of planet Earth. Jesus has the Divine Mind. We can communicate with Jesus on the celestial realm. The ultimate goal of achievement is toward higher levels of intelligence and perfection. In this life only advances made toward such perfection are never taken away from us in the spiritual world.

Karma

Live your life on a spiritual plane, of harmony, goodness and truth. You ride over death. You have overcome death. There is no need to reincarnate to come back. Your work is finished. Karma is erased and forgotten. Reincarnation – this occurs when you fail to let go of man-made conditions of creed or dogma that have been imposed on you. You need to learn. Death may be overcome through round after round of Earthly experience.

Creation is eternal and mankind's creatures are always changing under the Universal Law of action and reaction. Cosmic law never allows life to run too far in a tangent. This law is polarized in equalization, balance and harmony. The law of truth existed before man had consciousness. Man's conscious knowledge of the truth can be compared against absolute truth to find how far up the ladder he has climbed.

The Message behind the Baird Spalding Journeys

1) I quote from the back cover of each volume which states;

'There is no question but these people have brought the light through the long ages and they prove their daily life and works that this light does exist just as it did thousands of years ago.'

Baird Spalding's description of his Far East travels have played a very important role in introducing to the Western World the knowledge that there are many Masters who are assisting and guiding the destinies of mankind. His encounters with the Masters present a dramatic enfoldment of spiritual teachings and episodes unparalleled in all of Western literature.

2) There are so many appearances of Jesus in his own body and papers of his teachings. Also so many other Grand Masters who can come and go in their physical/spiritual bodies and who live in the celestial realms with Jesus, like Emil, Emil's mother and family. To say I have shaken hands with Jesus and talked to him is wonderful.

3) The entire journeys and encounters with Jesus and the Grand Masters were predestined to happen.

4) The extraordinary demonstrations of:

body transfer — access to Universal Substance
thought transference — access to Universal Energy
levitation — instruction of achieving God inside us
healing and miracles — happenings which to us were miracles
pictures from the past — to the natives were everyday occurrences

5) From many different places the location of the lost cities in the Gobi Desert was found.

6) Intelligent man existed 230,000 BC. This is about the same time the increased functions of the brain due to its enlargement and syntax occurred; the ability to plan ahead and reason.

7) Will all the lost photographs and details of the journeys be found one day? Are the photos of Jesus in the Taw Cross Temple? Are some of the records in Darjeeling where they all had their last meeting to compare their findings? I doubt it. De Vorss, Baird Spalding's publishers, didn't receive them. Perhaps there are none.

Sir Jagadish Chandra Bose was a great scientist from the Bose Institute in Calcutta. When he died in 1937 Americans continued his experiments and said he was 80 years ahead of his time. He discovered Micro waves and energy patterns and levels running through flowers, animals and humans. His work on interference light properties came in useful when he photographed the spirit leaving the body. The spirit had form and intelligence. The physical body lost weight on death. On one occasion he put the body of one who was dying in a lead coffin and covered it in asbestos. He couldn't photograph the spirit leaving the body. 24 hours later he opened the coffin to find the spirit had gone back into the person, who regained consciousness and lived another 15 years.

On death the etheric aura lifts off and forms the mould which takes the spiritual body and the mind to build a new person. This takes one to three days. Soul and Spirit mean the same. The soul is the collective intelligence, wisdom and contact to higher dimensions through the crown chakra and heart centre.

The level of spiritual attainment never goes down. It continues with the spirit. As spirits become purified they can reincarnate on successfully better worlds to the point where they overcome imperfections and overcome the need for material connection with matter.

In Baird Spalding's Book One, Emil's mother declares, 'We live in the celestial realm with Jesus, a place where we know the real meaning of transfigurations, where we are able to commune with God, and see Him face to face.'

In the book *The Essence of Kabbalah* by Brian L Lancaster the phrase 'living soul' is called speaking soul. OnKelos says in the Kabbalah the real divine gift is the ability to form the sounds of speech and to use language to forge a relationship with God. God wants to speak to us. This goes back to God when He spoke to Moses. I believe this was the stimulus God gave to our brains to expand so we could have communication with Him, the ability to produce intelligent speech.

Do you believe in the laws of justice, love and charity that God has set standards for you to achieve purity, perfection, peace and love? We can have moral codes, standards which we would consider acceptable, without inviting God into the equation.

List of good intentions:

The law of freedom
The law of justice, love and charity
The law of equality
The law of progress
The law of preservation
The law of distraction
The law of labour
The law of worship
The law of nature

In the last 200 years most of these good intentions have been broken. When we examine the philosophical approach we come to the conclusion some philosophers have atheistic ideas, have no moral codes, and nothing we could call decent. Frederick W Nietzsche (1844 – 1900) was an example of someone opposing God (his greatest admirer was Adolf Hitler, a man in power to make himself God), that the way to enlightenment was self-satisfaction, the supremacy of man over his enemies, and the right to kill six million Jews and was responsible for the deaths of countless others. Stalin before him was no better – massacre of 20 millions – he was an atheist who raised his fist to God on his death bed.

The same can be said of the Japanese. While America sat around the negotiating table with the Japanese the American fleet was sunk in Pearl Harbour. What was the final outcome? A nuclear bomb on Hiroshima killing 150,000 people.

In China we watched as students gather in Tiananmen Square wanting freedom of speech. Many were killed. China has taken over Tibet with soldiers, massacres, temple and monasteries destroyed, for what reason? The ideology of dictatorship.

The same in Iraq – Saddam Hussein – a mad man, unscrupulous, kills, gases, tortures, even his own family, for his own wealth and importance, saying, 'I am above the law'. Saddam Hussein was a Sunni Muslim.

We have persecutions all over planet Earth. In Burma the Junta are killing thousands of monks, wars in Africa, even on our own doorstep in Europe. Death fear, anger, hatred, build up to the roots of evil and these radiations come from man's greed for wealth and power, dictators who are atheists. Aristotle said all philosophy begins with wonder, it must come to truth and destiny. As science advances so philosophers' thoughts advance and in this modern day and age scientific discoveries must influence the thoughts of philosophers. There is more trust in sciences and mathematics. Even the church has tried to influence philosophers and scientists to change their thoughts for their own personal gain.

Why have I mentioned all these things? There is a massive swing toward common belief in God in the World today, from Christians, Jews, Muslims and many others, where prayers are said to God, to Jesus Christ, to Mohammed, to Buddha and there is only one God. These positive vibrations of God are counteracting the negative vibes, counteracting atheism, and modern communication with world wide TV gives full voice to human rights. What is the message? Stop wars, any killings against God's children are evil. Jesus says love your enemies; we are all God's creatures. Peace should be everywhere. Stop fighting in Iraq, Afghanistan, and Africa, in Tibet, in Burma and in Palestine. Oppose atheism with the power of love.

Chapter Eleven

Conclusions

I.

1) Earth is an experimental laboratory for growing things. It is an example of how to operate ecology and shows that everything contributes to the whole by a gradual process of build up. When the time was right chimpanzee and man evolved.

2) Order came by design and not from chaos.

3) The common denominator is the beauty and diversity of creation. This came about by the laws of creation and ecology. Planet Earth could have been influenced by other planets. Design features could have been different. Only a small modification in chemistry and photosynthesis could have produced a red planet where grass, trees and nature are predominantly Red. DNA is probably five billion years old. Could it have been altered in the past?

4) God expanded man's brain so we could speak to God and God could speak to man.

5) God has a purpose for mankind to share in His beauty of creation and creation is continuous.

6) The new brain was fully formed 300,000 years ago. Now it is up to man to use it in its full capacity. God will further expand our energy level of consciousness so we can see and communicate with the next life.

7) A superior race existed 230,000 years ago living in 3 cities in the then fertile Gobi Desert. Man lived close to God, could communicate with God, could access Universal Substance for every need, and live in a spiritual plane of existence.

8) This spiritual body never dies and you take it with you into the

next life to achieve perfection as part of God's love and plan for us.

9) Some people have been given special gifts to move intelligence and understanding forwards.

10) Everything has its own vibrational energy level. Matter comes out of energy when you lower that particular vibrational energy level. In my diagram of creation from the Divine Principle downwards, music or sound vibration features in the beginning of creation. That is why I love playing the piano. I am playing with the sound of creation.

11) Sound wave energy can create particles to assume certain shapes.

12) Sound waves can be used in healing in many ways.

13) Every organ of the body has its own vibrational energy level and sends signals to the brain which co-ordinate to health of the whole. Each organ is represented by a chakra, so under-energised chakras can be energized by the light of the Divine Spirit of God to restore health.

14) Jesus not only showed the way to enlightenment 2000 years ago, but He is here today to help everyone that calls on His name in true belief. Then he will give you the gifts of the Holy Spirit, so we can be healers like Jesus.

15) Jesus said, 'When the heavens were opened unto Me, I saw the law of expression, whereby ideas conceived in the Divine Mind are made into form. All forms may be transformed or changed in form through a change of consciousness in regard to it.'

16) The way forward is World Peace. There is only one God who is pure love.

I leave you with this thought:

I saw the door to heaven was open and God writing a message 'Wanted good teachers for overseas appointments, no salary, payment by abundance of God's love.'

II. Books I recommend you to read:

1) 6 volumes. *Life and Teaching of the Masters of the Far East* by Baird T Spalding DeVorss & Co Publisher, PO Box 1389, Camarillo, CA 93011 – 1389, USA www.devorss.com ISBN 0875 165389

2) *Need to Know* Christianity from its ancient roots to its modern relevance by Peter Graystone. Published by Collins ISBN 978-0-00-7261161

3) *The Illustrated Book of Sacred Scriptures* by Timothy Freke ISBN 0722 535682

4) *The Elements of Meditation* by David Fontana ISBN 1862 04036-2

5) *Mind to Mind* by Betty Shine 0552 135787 A Corgi Book

Several other books of Mind Magic 0552 136719

6) *The Egyptian Book of the Dead* by Dr Ramses Seleem ISBN 184181 109-2

7) *The Essence of Kabbalah* by Brian L Lancaster ISBN 1-84 193-388-6

8) *A Practical Guide to Hands on Healing* by Jack Angelo ISBN 184 181-149-1

9) *World Religions* by Dr Ian Barnes ISBN 978 184 573 356-8

10) *Crystal Power, Crystal Healing, the Complete Handbook* by Michael Gienger ISBN 071 372677-6

11) *The Miracle of Colour Healing, AURA-Soma Therapy as the Mirror of the Soul* by Vicky Wall ISBN 085030895X

12) *The Healing Journey* by Matthew Manning ISBN 07499 22443

13) *A Guide to Meditation* by Lorraine Turner ISBN 0-75257-198-2

14) *The Dalai Lama's Book of Wisdom* ISBN 13978072253955-2

III. The Sixth Miracle

On Monday 12th October, 2009 I went to Church in Paignton in Devon. There were about 60 people in the congregation. The Vicar Denise Vandenberg pointed at me and said, 'John I have Jesus with me. He has a message for you. This is his message. 'The crises of confidence is over, you will have no more problems."

Jesus accessed my brain. I was totally under his control. We have cells in our brain which receive messages from the Divine Mind. When Jesus chose his disciples he said, 'follow me'. Jesus accessed their brains, and they followed him.

The thought is very powerful. It preceded the spoken words by a million year. It travels at vast speeds outside of known science. It has been estimate to travel at 370 million miles per second. It is how we communicate in the universe. The bible starts in the beginning was the word. This is a mistranslation. In the beginning was the thought. The word was made holy when God spoke to Moses 3400 years ago. God has many prophets in the bible. I quote from 1 Corinthians 12 verses 4–11

'4. There are different kinds of gifts , but the same Spirit. 5. There are different kinds of service, but the same Lord. 6. There are different kinds of working, but the same God works all of them in all men. 7. Now to each one the manifestation of the Spirit is given for the common good. 8. To one there is given through the spirit the message of wisdom, to another the message of knowledge by means of the same spirit. 9. to another faith by the same Spirit, to another gifts of healing by that one spirit. 10. to another miraculous powers, to another prophecy, to another distinguishing between spirits, to another speaking in different kinds of tongues, and to still another the interpretation of tongues. 11. All these are the work of one and the same Spirit, and he give them to each one, just as he determines.'

It is the same God that works in all men. Underlying all religions it is the same story. 'Of myself I can do nothing. It is God inside me that does the work. This is the work of the Divine Spirit.'

We all have a purpose to achieve. In John gospel he says Jesus told us many other things which are not written in this gospel, enough to fill every book in the world. What are those things? I will mention a few of them. Jesus said 'when the heavens were opened unto him, he saw the law of expression whereby ideas conceived in the Divine mind are made into form. All forms may be transformed or changed in form through a change of consciousness in regard to it.'

IV. Jesus told his disciples that they must

1. Be pure in heart, for the pure in heart shall see God.
2. Achieve perfection in everything you do.
3. Be Peaceful to all people and animals.
4. Love everybody and everything that is good.
5. Learn how to get God inside to work through you in channeling divine spiritual energy for healing. Then you can heal the sick.
6. Learn how miracles are performed e.g. walking on water. With the power of positive thought you see rock and you walk on rock.
7. Learn the nature of cosmic energy; how everything has a vibrational energy rate and how matter comes from energy when you lower its vibrational energy rate.
8. Understand the power of transmission of the thought process.
9. Develop beautiful thoughts for transmission.
10. Collect past events and focus them to a point to review them.
11. Believe there is an abundance all about us of universal substance to satisfy mans every need.
12. Know there is an abundance of universal energy for mans every need.
13. Believe there are universal laws that can never be changed.
14. Understand the nature of the Divine path can never be changed. When it deviates too far from the straight it will be drawn back into line.
15. Commit to afterlife or spiritual life.

V. New Scientific News

In May 2010 Scientists announce a major breakthrough, moving knowledge another leap ahead. They have made a living cell nicknamed Synthia.

I wrote earlier in my book that God gave us a large brain so we could have an understanding of the universe and share His creation. It is only right now that we share in creation, provided we obey the rules for creation. A good desire is God's desire. Love forms a part of God's creation.

What do you want to create? Maybe we can create for the benefit of medicine, to heal sick people. Maybe we can create for industry, for example, an alternative form of energy. If you can create one living cell, you can create a million. You must decide how much information your one cell will carry. Everything is made from energy. Creation is continuous, expanding and concentrating, and through reduced vibrations, condensing into form.

Can energy be put into 'blocks of energy' for creation and through reduced vibrations condense into form for use to stamp our cells with their characteristics? Insects can home in on different smells, shapes, temperatures and background environment. We see different colours as each colour had a different wavelength. Scientists have failed to understand that in the world about us, everything goes to make up a whole, and nothing stands in isolation. We are only one part of a great body of earth's creation, and maybe part of the creation of the great cosmos, full of different creations.

Years ago I realised how important the background environment plays when I was doing regression techniques in hypnosis. I would take a person back to when they were five years old, and ask them to write their name. Mother would be present to confirm the signature was correct against writings from that age.

'Now you are only five years old and you are going to write your name.'

This is what happened. The posture changed. The legs splayed and arms moved apart. The pencil was held differently. The face moved closer to the paper. The body was lowered toward the paper. The motion of the pencil was different. You asked the child for a signature at five years old. What did you get? The brain had recorded every move of the body and noted the environment about you at that time, as well as producing the signature. Everything is 'part of a whole'. Nothing is in isolation.

At the end of May is the Chelsea Flower Show. From all over the world come exotic flowers, plants, vegetables. Here is the beauty and diversity of creation I talked about the floral pavilion, full of colours, quite unimaginable, with many new varieties. Orchids have developed a beautiful cup for insects to pollinate. Is there anywhere a greater love story on planet earth between insects and flowers? Why don't you start your creation of living cells with a love cup for insects to pollinate. Play beautiful music to your creation. Write beautiful poetry to your creation. Surround your creation with love. Creation cannot stand alone in isolation of other forces.

If you wish to take your creation further and animate it, you are totally responsible for looking after it. You must always project good thoughts and in a good environment. Can your creation go wrong? Yes it can. This is an example. If you had bad negative thoughts and wished your creation to freeze, you then become the creation under the universal laws of cause and effect, and you would freeze.

There are many millions of creators in the universe. It is God's wish for us to share in his love of creation. Do flowers talk to each other and do they share energies? Certainly they share he sun's energy. I believe they share each other's energy.

In the mountains flowers produce larger cups, so insects can find them to pollinate. Who tells them to make bigger cups? It is programmed into them.

I wish we knew all God's universal laws that can never be changed. I don't expect we would understand them. When human beings have gone far enough in their creation of creatures, the Great Absolute Law of Truth takes a hand in bringing them face to face with the original plan. We see that cosmic laws never allows life to run too far in a tangent. This law is always polarised in equalization, balance and harmony. Man's consciousness in the product of a large brain and the ability to plan ahead and reason. Other creatures have consciousness but to a lesser extent and with no ability to plan ahead. Before man's consciousness, before all neurological connections produce any consciousness and awareness of any sort was present, *absolute truth* existed. When the law of Truth comes to consciousness, it will erase all that humanity has ever thought erroneously. Cosmic Absolute Law must be fully satisfied.

If we all loved God and loved our enemies, there would be no evil in the world. How difficult it is to love your enemies. I sometimes have bad thoughts against those that have harmed me.

International Peace Day is September 21st. This is the day for everyone to put down their arms and pray for world peace. Then we can have *heaven on earth*. When Jesus talked to me he totally accessed my brain. I was totally under his control. If everyone on earth was in peace with each other and loved God, perhaps the reverse could happen that is we could access God.

Our brain is in two halves joined together at the Pyramids. It acts as one brain, but the left hand side is given over to logical thinking, the right hand side, inspirational thinking. God can know our every thought. The church recognizes evil forces which can possess people and access their brain activities. Both the Anglican and Roman Catholic Churches have Bishops appointed to exercise evil spirits.

Have 'Fallen Angels' the power to create evil things? Why does the denge mosquito, aedes aegyptic, with its haemorrhage strain (There are 4 strains) have the power to kill 30% of its victims with a single bite? These are questions we do not know the answers. Only to say, we form only one part of a great body of earth's creation, and maybe the denge mosquito wasn't programmed to bite us, but things went wrong with its programming. At times we seem to be fighting new viruses, having overcome smallpox, which killed a third of the world's population, now to find mutations and the ever urgent need to control viruses and epidemics. Modern science is finding answers to our questions. God and sciences are working together for us, that our researches and knowledge provide the answers to our questions, provided we incorporate love into our answers.

What does science tell us about creation? In 1927, 29 scientists met at Brussels to discuss the Quantum Theory. The atom consists of central nucleus with electrons orbiting at different distances, held in place by forces similar to our earth and planets orbiting the sun, the gravitational force. The Copenhagen theory was adopted. The exploding of the atom bomb in 1944 confirmed some predictions. Einstein tried to find a universal theory to incorporate both Quantum mechanics and his theory of relativity, $E=mc^2$. It has since been discovered. G.U.T. = Grand Unified Theory. Quantum mechanics has the answers. Q.E.D. = Quantum Electro Dynamics.

At very high energy levels (which we cannot produce in the laboratory) the forces of electromagnetic and weak forces and the strong nuclear force would have the same strength and would be different aspects of the same force called The Grand Unification Energy. Many different particles can change at different energy levels. At the Cern Tunnel (European Energy Centre for nuclear research) particles are made to accelerate and collisions occur. The results are recorded. New particles form, sometimes appearing in two places at the same time. Everything in the universe, including light and gravity, can be described in terms of particles and the wave particle duality. Protons and neutrons have been found to be made up of smaller particles, called Quarks.

There are six different types of Quarks. A proton and a neutron are made of three Quarks each. These particles display spin. The strong nuclear force holds the Quarks together in the proton and the neutron. Protons and neutrons make up the mass of ordinary matter. Evidence suggests there was a big bang 13.7 million years ago, and predictions before this time are impossible. In the laboratory, matter has been made which exists in two places at the same time. Is there a parallel universe alongside our own? 3400 years ago, God said to Moses the universe is made from ten different dimensions. Science is proving this to be so.

VI. A Two hour DVD film about this book

This film starts in Brixham, visiting St Mary's Anglican Church and All Saints Church and continues in my house with a précis of my story and meeting Jesus.

In section 2, the story is told in more detail with shots filmed in the Caribbean, and messages from Jesus.

Section 3 takes you to Tibet, to explore creation from the divine principle downwards and climbing the ladder to God within. It introduces you to Buddhism.

In section 4, I travelled to Nepal, Kathmandu and to Bhutan. Conclusions to teach you about inner peace.

In the last section, we visit the ancient church in Hambie Village, Southampton, and show evidence of Christianity arriving there in 500AD from the Benedictine Monks, with conclusions of recommended books to buy.

DVDs are available from John Cawsey, 34 Overgang, Brixham, South Devon, TQ5 8AP, priced at £6.50 including postage and packaging.